YOU'RE NOT SPECIAL
BUT YOU'RE ENOUGH.

Overcoming Imposter Syndrome and Stepping into Your Worthiness

By **Jillian Parekh** B.A., M.A., and **Master Coach**

Dedication

For my family - Mom, Dad, Tallon, Larissa.
My first home.

And for Dustin.
My forever home.

I would not be me without you.

Thank you.
I love you.

About the Author

Jill Parekh is a Master Business & Mindset Coach, and coaches women on overcoming imposter syndrome and stepping into the identity of who they're meant to be.

You can find Jill on Instagram @yourcoachjill, listen to The From Imposter to Empowered Podcast on most podcast streaming platforms, and visit her website www.jillianparekh.com for her coaching programs, blog, and more.

Jill lives in Ontario, Canada with her fiancé, Dustin, their dog, Hugo, and their cat, Chester. She is a full-time Master Coach, loves One Tree Hill, orange chocolate, reading & writing, the colour pink, and the ocean. She is an advocate for women with invisible disabilities, as she herself has ADHD and a stuttering disability.

You're Not Special is Jill's first self-published book. There are mindset resources and exercises all throughout this book, and you can find them at www.jillianparekh.com/yns-book

Table of Contents

What is Imposter Syndrome?	1
You're Not Special	7
What If You Were Wrong?	15
Your Inner Imposter	23
Your Thoughts are a Dialogue, Not a Ted Talk	25
How to Stop Overthinking	34
The Song of Your People AKA The Stupid Fucking Beliefs You Picked Up From Your Lineage	36
You're Not Too Sensitive, Bitch	40
Reframing the Past Doesn't Mean Changing It	48
Everything You Do is to Avoid a Feeling	50
"Should" is Just Shame with Sugar on Top	60
Disappointment is A (Shitty) Part of Life	67
Perfectionism Only Sounds Good on a Resume	71
Rejection: It's Going to Feel Like You're Dying Even Though You're Not	78

You Could Never Be Found Out	85
Failure is an Illusion	87
Self-Acceptance is The Bare Fucking Minimum	90
How to Accept Yourself	98
Safety & Worthiness are Feelings You Have, Not Things You Achieve	99
Safe & Comfortable Are Two Different Things	106
The Debilitating Fear of Being Seen	108
You Are Not Bad	115
You Are Just Enough, Even When You Are Too Much	118
Facing Feedback and Criticism	121
Don't Stay Small to Make Others Comfortable	125
This, or Something Better	127
Feeling Worthy is an Ongoing Identity Crisis	132
Becoming The Worthy Woman	135
Beliefs You Can Borrow to Lily Pad Your Way to Worthiness	138
How to Be A Sensitive Bad Bitch	139

Your Journey to Worthiness Begins Today	141
The Good Avocados	146
It's All Happening	149
You Are Good Enough	151
You Get to Decide That You're Good Enough	153
Now What?	155
Welcome Home	157
Acknowledgements	*158*
Sources	*160*

What is Imposter Syndrome?

The first time I Googled imposter syndrome, it was during a two-week on-campus residency for my Master's.

I sat in the classroom with my fellow students, many of them quite older than me *(they loved it when I reminded them of this)*. I overheard a classmate tell someone else that she knew someone who was on the waitlist, but they didn't get in.

"Wait", I said. "They didn't let just anybody into this program?" As if I climbed in the fucking window and parked myself at a desk, refusing to move.

I typed in "Feels like I'm faking it" into Google that night, huddled in my dorm room, my face illuminated by the blue light. The clock said something like 1:00 a.m. or 1:05 a.m. I couldn't sleep because of the anxiety of being "found out" that week, meeting all my new classmates, and having to complete assignments & group projects. *(I would come to find out that the feeling of being a fraud is about 100x stronger when you're doing something new).*

Google will tell you that imposter syndrome is the persistent internalized fear of being revealed as a fraud[1].

But after coaching and teaching hundreds of clients within my coaching practice how to overcome imposter syndrome, I see it for what it really is.

The feeling of being unworthy.

Imposter syndrome is not just for the corporate or business world. It can actually be incredibly personal and incredibly debilitating.

There are similarities, patterns of behavior, traits, characteristics, and other nuances that I see with *all* of my clients, across their careers, businesses, in their relationships, and in their overall sense of self.

Here are some thoughts, feelings, and behaviors that may be consistent with feeling like a fraud:

- Discrediting your work and accomplishments, providing rationale for why you didn't play a big part in creating them
- Thinking the work you produce is below average, and could be better if you tried harder
- Automatically assuming most people know more/better than you
- Believing everyone has everything figured out, and you do not
- Disregarding compliments or thinking people are lying to you when they compliment you
- Believing your worth is based on what you can produce/will accomplish in the future, so you

---

[1] *Feel like a fraud? American Psychological Association, 2013.*

overwork and overdo
- Being unable to realistically assess your skills or competence
- Over-sensitivity to rejection & criticism
- A persistent fear of failure or looking stupid
- Feeling on edge, like you're going to be "found out" if you make a mistake
- Internalizing mistakes or failures much more than internalizing successes
- Thinking nobody knows the "real" you
- A deep sense of shame and/or embarrassment for the thoughts you have, the things you do, and just for being who you are

After six years of education & experience in the field of psychology and conflict, and five years of coaching hundreds of women on overcoming their inner imposter, I found that at its core, the feeling of being a fraud boils down to **feeling unworthy**.

Feeling not good enough.

Being wrong, incapable, insufficient.

It is an overall feeling that attaches itself to your identity.

When I go on podcasts or do interviews, I have some standard advice to get you started:

1. Don't identify with your thoughts; separate yourself from your inner imposter.
2. Track your accomplishments.

3. Tell someone you feel like a fraud. Imposter syndrome hides in shame.

These are surface-level strategies. Ones I offer to people who want a quick fix, a simple *introduction* to something that I believe needs to be taken deeper if it is truly affecting your life.

But how do you change your thinking when all you've ever known is self-loathing and you had a critical parent growing up?

How do you track your accomplishments when you genuinely think you don't have any, or when you think that the ones you *do* have suck ass?

How do you tell someone you feel like a fraud when you're a raging perfectionist and would rather *die* than admit to someone you think you don't know what you're doing?

Surface-level strategies never penetrate the root. And if there's one thing about me, I need to know the HOW and the WHY about everything. My mind, body, and soul need to be on board when I'm making changes to my life.

And you're the same. If imposter syndrome wasn't internally wreaking havoc on your life and your future success, you wouldn't have picked up this book.

How am I qualified to help you through imposter syndrome?

I have a Bachelor's degree in Sexuality, Marriage & Family studies, which are primary-level counselling practices and concepts. I then moved onto a Master's in Conflict Analysis and Management. When I became a coach, I became Master certified in neuro linguistic programming (NLP), which is the observation of how our subjective experience creates our patterns, actions, and behaviors. I was certified as a Master Clinical Hypnotherapist and a Master EFT Tapping

Practitioner. And finally, I became a facilitator of Breathwork, which is a somatic healing modality using the breath to regulate the nervous system and heal past trauma and patterns of wounding.

In my coaching practice today, I blend psychology, subconscious mind tools, and somatic tools to help my clients break through their feelings of imposter syndrome, reframe and release their past experiences, silence their inner critic, shift their thoughts and belief patterns, and ultimately, feel worthy and good enough to have the businesses, the careers, and the lives that they want.

One might say that I'm *overqualified*, and I have to be honest - a lot of my education and certification was done out of the need to feel capable, qualified, and good enough. Those qualifications gave me temporary relief and something to rely on when I felt insecure. But I had to do my own work around worthiness, belief in myself, and confidence in order to feel capable, confident, and good enough everyday, so I could do the work I was meant to do.

I do this for women who have never felt worthy, because it's what I needed so desperately.

I was undiagnosed with ADHD for most of my life and I have a stutter that developed when I began speaking. I never grew out of it, much to my dismay, as stutters are hereditary (just like ADHD) and my dad had both as a child - but he grew out of his stutter. My stutter affected my self-worth so much growing up *(and still does to some degree)*. I felt outcasted, ugly, stupid, and unworthy because I couldn't communicate the way others could.

When I was 29, I finally went to get diagnosed with ADHD after being on the ADHD side of TikTok for a year and a half, and I also found research linking speech impediments to ADHD.

I finally understood why my brain functioned the way it did. When you begin to understand why you think the things you think, why you feel the way you feel, and why you act the way you act *(these three things are all working together, by the way)* there is a brand-new level of compassion and awareness that comes with it.

You're no longer defective or weird or whatever else you told yourself. You can now move forward and manage the brain you have and the life you were given. You become the hero instead of the victim.

You may be acting like a victim of your circumstances. You might believe that there really is something wrong with you, you really don't know what you're doing, and the fear and anxiety from failing or fucking up or being rejected keeps you in an endless loop of inaction and self-loathing, or maybe even taking-action-while-you-cringe-because-your-worth-is-rooted-in-productivity-and-achieviements and self-loathing.

I'm in the latter camp, if you were wondering.

All this to say, I came to a realization one night, in the bath *(where I do all my best thinking and idea creation),* wondering why I wasn't getting the results I wanted in my business. Are you ready for this ground-breaking revelation?

You're Not Special

That might hurt your feelings a bit when you first read it. You might think, WTF Jill, my mommy told me I was special. And of course, you are. To your mom, of course. My mom thinks I'm special too. Hi Mom. I wrote a book. Tell me I'm smart and pretty.

Moms' aside - you're not special, and I'm not special.

There is nothing so special, unique, substantial, terrible, or shameful, about *you*, that makes it so you can't be the person you want to be and have the life that you want.

There is no law, or scripture written in stone, or absolute truth that [insert your name here] cannot have what she desires.

You're not that special. **But you believe that you are**. And you might be like how I used to be, who had a desire to be revered and respected and be seen as so cute and unique and AMAZING, but also you low-key don't like yourself and think you're a huge fraud so even if you were loved and respected and seen as special, you'd be found out. And this makes you super sensitive to failure and rejection because then it would confirm all your worst fears about yourself, so you literally feel like you're scraping by at any given moment.

No? Just me?

For reasons you feel certain of, you have subconsciously decided that you are unworthy of everything that you want, and that's why you don't have it. Maybe you tell yourself it's because you came from a small town where you're two steps away from spitting on your ex-boyfriend who hangs a ballsack from his truck *(you dodged a bullet there, trust me)*.

Maybe you tell yourself it's because your parents didn't have any money growing up and you think you're doomed to their fate of credit card debt and living paycheck to paycheck.

Maybe you tell yourself it's because you're first generation and your family would simply roll over and *die* if you didn't become a doctor or a lawyer, even though you can't imagine doing something like that for the next 40 years.

Here's what else it could be:

It's because you had a run in with the mean girl on the playground who thought it was hilarious that a boy said he liked you. Why would *he* like *you?* she asked.

It's because you had a teacher who made you feel stupid.

It's because you spent a little too much of your scholarship money at the mall when you went to college and ended up eating rice and beans by second semester, and you've felt irresponsible with money ever since, despite our generation being crippled by student debt, an unrealistic housing market, and record-high inflation.

It's because you had experience after experience, and a lot of those experiences made you feel not good enough.

So you decided that you were.

You decided you were unworthy, most likely at a deep unconscious level, leaving you unsatisfied with each milestone you hit and experience you have, because you simply do not feel good enough.

Unworthiness is at the root of imposter syndrome.

But I need you to know…..you **are** worthy. The work is never trying to figure out if you are, it's finally **believing** that you are. You are already good enough and capable enough to go after and have the things that you want.

That's great news, Jill, but why don't I *feel* good enough?

We'll get to the feeling part later. But I also think that you may be reading those words right now, and forgetting that despite you being good and perfect and worthy the way you are….it doesn't mean that hardships, negative emotions and thoughts, and shitty experiences won't happen to you.

I'm worthy of being a successful coach, but I've still had to process refunds and run after clients for payments.

I'm worthy of being treated with respect, but I've still experienced quite a lot of *disrespect*, like when my fiancé eats my East Side Mario's leftovers.

You being worthy does not void you of the human experience. Stop asking yourself why things are happening to you, why they are the way they are, and why nothing ever works out for you. Just because you decided you're a fairy princess doesn't mean you won't have shitty days or people trying to knock your crown off because of their own shit.

Stop thinking that every experience that sparks something less than joy means something about you and why you're not good enough.

It's the equivalent of stomping your feet in the grocery store because your mom wouldn't buy you a chocolate bar at checkout. Yes, your mom still loves you, she just also pays for you to go to the dentist, and you're getting McDonald's on the way home, anyway.

Yes, you are still worthy and capable and good enough, but right now, you're having a human experience - and that's okay. It's okay if someone wants a refund. It's okay if someone disrespects you and you have to set some boundaries. It's okay if something didn't go the way you envisioned it. It's okay if you didn't hit your goal in time. It's okay that you didn't get the exact position you wanted.

Nothing has to mean anything. You get to decide what experiences mean. You get to decide how to process the experience of someone asking for a refund or someone disrespecting you. You get to decide, because you are the person who has to live inside your mind.

Like forgiveness. You don't forgive people for them. You forgive them for you. So you can move forward and feel better. More on that later, too.

Essentially, what I'm saying is that when you feel confident and worthy, you are not denying that bad things exist or that negative emotions will happen. You go through the human experience, trusting yourself and knowing that everything will work out the way it's supposed to - because worthiness is your baseline.

Foundational worthiness looks like:

- A loving & compassionate inner dialogue → Being in a loving, committed relationship to yourself, and empowering yourself with your thoughts.

- Trusting yourself & your decision-making → Knowing that you have your own back and you're making the best decisions for yourself.
- Discernment between what's anxiety/fear and your intuition → Being attuned to your body that helps you make the distinction.
- Confidence in your unique capabilities → Believing you bring value to the world [bonus points if you believe that no one can do it like you can]
- And lastly, emotional resilience → The capability to feel & process your emotions and not make the negative ones mean anything.

Here's the thing - you were not born with any of that.

It has to be learned.

I do believe that we are born worthy, live worthy , and die worthy.

And I do believe that most, if not all of us, stumble through life and experience it abruptly, like a bull in a china shop. We are unaware, unassuming, and we break a lot of shit along the way.

We break our innate worthiness. Or someone else breaks it for us.

We have parents that abandon us, lovers that betray us, friends that exclude us.

We have schools that reject us, and jobs that mistreat us, and buses that roll past our stop when we're standing *literally right there*.

We also have times of self-sabotage. When we know better, but do the opposite anyways. We fuck up, say the wrong thing, forget something important, hurt someone we love.

So that's why I'm not going to preach to you about how you should have always believed you were worthy, and now you're a self-help junkie who has to read this book to come back to it.

I'm here to help you build a foundation of worthiness for the person you are right now.

You may have lost it at some point - but now, we're going to take it back.

Because here's what I think:

Your UNworthiness is a rite of passage *(and this should help you not to dwell on it).*

Yep, that's right, I think it is completely and totally okay that you don't feel good enough or that you feel like you never have.

I think that most, if not all of us, were born worthy, and then stumbled through life - first, as little sponges that absorbed everything in our environment and the people in it, from thoughts about religion and money to attachments in relationships and whether or not your family drinks milk at dinner.

Then, we've all had experiences that led us to believe we were unworthy, not good enough, not smart enough, not capable enough, not creative enough. We develop habits and coping mechanisms that protect us or perpetuate our consistent thought patterns & feelings of being unworthy.

And then, we wake up.

This is a common term in spiritual circles. It essentially means to go from being unconscious and unaware to becoming conscious and aware.

This is how I think it happens:

I think that a lot of our childhoods and younger adolescence, when our brains are still developing, neural pathways are being solidified, and we're doing more absorbing than observing - it's fuzzy. It feels like I was in my body, but not fully conscious of everything around me.

I was unconscious. I was absorbing, but not observing.

And now, I'm awake. And you are too or you wouldn't be reading this. Or you're my friends & family, who I basically held hostage and made them promise to read it.

This half of my life, the half where I feel like I'm fully conscious, felt like it began when I walked into a therapist's office in January 2019 *(new year, new neural pathways am I right?)*

It's like I woke up and was like what the fuck? Who the fuck am I? What the fuck am I doing? What does this all mean?

An existential crisis, if you will.

But it's more than that. As I began my self-healing, self-discovery journey, it meant I had to unpack every thought about myself, every feeling I stuffed down and numbed out in hopes of it going away, and every experience that I triggered me, traumatized me, or just simply fed into a belief that I'd been carrying with me my entire life.

When I was a little girl, I called the yard in the front of our house my Magical Forest. I used to talk to God, hang out with my unicorn, Rainbow Sparkles, and take the elevator up to heaven and back down again to Earth. Mind you, we weren't religious in the slightest, and I went to a public school. I also used to write so many stories and poems, and then would go to my Omi's and type them up because they had a computer.

But everyone would say you don't make any money as an author, so I stopped writing. I stopped believing in a higher power and magic and I crushed my creativity and spirit with logic, realism, sarcasm, and self-deprecation.

I grew up, and because of societal pressures and norms, ingrained familial beliefs and patterns, experiences of exclusion and ridicule, doubt, fear, and rejection - I lost my feelings of worthiness. I never felt good enough, and I had a stuttering disability that affected every part of my life, including making me feel like I had nothing to offer the world.

Now, you're reading my book. I have a coaching business that would never have existed if I didn't believe in myself, believe in a higher power that unequivocally has my back, and believe in the magic of my dreams coming true.

I'm not special, though. I'm just as fucked up and weird and awkward and amazing as you. And that's the point. No one is so special enough that they can't change their lives for the better. No one is so special that things are just meant to be shitty for them, and that's it.

It doesn't matter how old you are, what you've done, who you've been - you can choose to become conscious, right now.

Are you awake?

WHAT IF YOU WERE WRONG?

There is a societal norm of moral superiority when someone says what they mean and means what they say. When they walk the walk and talk the talk.

But the reality is...

You, my friend, are a hypocrite.

We all are.

We are all walking, talking, contradictions in a meat sack. All day, everyday, you are thinking thoughts that crash into each other like dumbasses on Highway 401. You are declaring to your friends at dinner that you're never going back to your ex, while you're secretly texting him under the table. You tell your therapist how calm and collected you've been, and then on your way home, you call someone a fucking idiot because they didn't use their turn signal.

You are constantly living in a state of thinking one thing, doing another thing, believing one thing, but not in this context, and I really think this, but I *feel* like this...

It feels like a mess in your head, constantly.

This isn't a problem, but you believe it is.

In psychology terms, this is called cognitive dissonance[2] the mental discomfort from holding conflicting ideas or opinions.

The idea here is that when you have conflicting thoughts or beliefs, it is uncomfortable. It makes you unsure and anxious. And it's usually because your beliefs/thoughts are clashing with your behaviour and what's happening in your physical reality - or vice versa.

As an example: You write in your journal everyday that you're ready for clients and abundance to flow through your business, but you have this little voice in your head that thinks it's not possible. So because you have that nagging feeling, you tap into the incongruence more than you tap into what you're trying to create *(because you're a human and humans are difficult AND they're wired to focus on the negative)*.

The only reason why holding conflicting thoughts and beliefs are uncomfortable, is because you think it shouldn't be happening.

Just like our huge range of emotions or difficult life experiences - they can be extremely painful, yes. But what makes them more painful is questioning and resisting their existence in the first place.

You have been conditioned to believe that you should stand for something fiercely, and only stand for that. That you need to believe in something so strongly and never sway your opinion. We live in a world where if you say something, someone can probably go back and screenshot it or record it and then hold it against you in 30 years when you inevitably change your

---

[2] *Cognitive Dissonance Theory by Saul McLeod, 2018*

opinion, or gain some life experience that knocks you in the other direction.

Think political parties, human rights issues, beliefs about wealth - all very polarized issues that demand you side with one or the other.

Research on the human brain revealed a concept called neuroplasticity[3], which refers to the lifelong capacity of the brain to change and rewire itself in response to stimulation of learning and experience. There is also evidence of neurogenesis, which is the ability to create new neurons and connections between neurons throughout a lifetime.

Meaning, that your brain is going to change over the course of your lifetime. Your thoughts, beliefs, ideas, opinions - everything you form with your little prefrontal cortex - will inevitably change over time.

My point in saying all of this and backing it up with the science-y stuff - is yes, you *can* change your thoughts.

You can change how you think about yourself.

You can change how you think about your business, your career, your bitchy mother-in-law *(fortunately for me I can't relate to that one),* your ability to create, your purpose in this world - you can shift the way you think about literally anything and everything.

But only if you want to.

Only if you believe it's possible.

AND, you have to make peace with the fact that you are never going to be fully congruent in your thoughts,

---

[3] *The SharpBrains Guide to Brain Fitness by Fernandez, Michelon, and Chapman, 2013*

beliefs, feelings, and behaviors. The manifestation gurus are going to HATE this - but I believe, as an overthinker whose thoughts run a million miles a minute...Full congruence with every positive, abundant thought in the direction you're trying to create is optimistic, but unrealistic. And believing you need to be 100% congruent with something to make it happen leads to a lot of beating yourself up and a lot of fear that the 10% of incongruency you have is going to fuck everything up.

There are days where you're going to believe the sun shines out of your ass and everyone needs to bow at your feet, and then days where you will feel *like* ass, without the sun shining out of it.

On both days, you are worthy.

On both days, you are good enough.

That is the point of creating a foundation of worthiness. To come back to it, even when you feel like ass. To have conflicting thoughts about yourself and think, "This is normal, I have a human brain."

We are all messy and imperfect. We are all stumbling through our lives and hoping no one catches on that we're winging pretty much everything that we're doing.

You are capable and worthy right now.

Whether you believe it or not.

My job is to help you truly and sincerely believe it, down to your core. And that starts with that messy brain and those conflicting thoughts of yours.

Okay, so you know how I said you *can* change your thoughts?

It might be a little difficult at first, because of these two things:

Your Conscious Critical Faculty[4],

And;

Confirmation Bias[5].

Your Conscious Critical Faculty (CCF) is a filter inside of your brain, and it is solely based on the information you received as a child and from the environment you were raised in. As you grew up, it was solidified by your experiences of what was right and what was wrong (but again, only based on what the people around you *believed* was right or wrong). This means that your CCF will most likely reject information that you are unfamiliar with or information that does not align with your beliefs, even if your beliefs are that the sky is purple and the Toronto Maple Leafs don't suck.

Your CCF takes all of your own personal knowledge and experience, and uses it as a compass for when new information comes in. For example, if you see someone saying how you can make a million dollars in 30 days, you'd immediately think "No, I can't".

Here's where I tell you that your CCF is filtering information based on your own perceived limitations.

If you don't have a lived experience of something happening, your CCF defaults to what you know for sure - it's not possible for you. And then you have what you believe is or isn't possible for you, made more desolate by how unworthy and not good enough you feel.

So how do you override your CCF when it comes to achieving goals and accomplishing things outside of what you used to believe was possible for you?

---

[4] *The Conscious Critical Faculty, by Terence Watts*
[5] *How Confirmation Bias Works, by Iqra Noor, 2020*

You've already done the first thing, which is becoming aware that your brain has this filter and that it is automatic based *only on what you know to be true.* There is not one person who has the same CCF backlog that you have. This is liberating, not limiting. The only thing that stands between you and what you want are your *thoughts.*

Let's put it into action. Your second step is, when you have thoughts of "I can't do that" or "That's not possible", catch those thoughts. Question them. Do you only think that this thing is impossible because *you* haven't achieved it? Has somebody else? Why are you any different? Question the fuck out of yourself. Remember - a messy brain is A-OK. Conflicting thoughts are A-OK.

Now, similarly, we have confirmation bias, which is a psychology term. This is when your brain actively seeks out or only pays attention to information that confirms your current thoughts and beliefs.

So yeah, if you believe you're not good enough, your brain is going to latch onto past experiences and reasons as to why you're not good enough.

If you feel like a fraud when it comes to your business or your career, your brain will take all of your accomplishments, your relevant experiences, and any positive feedback, and will either rationalize it as to why it's not good enough or negate it all together.

Like when your boss or a client gives you an amazing review, but one piece of critical feedback - and you spin out. Perfectionism is at play here too, but for the sake of this argument, confirmation bias when you don't feel good enough will have you latch onto the piece of critical feedback and negate everything that was good. You might even go as far as to believe that everything good that they said about you wasn't true.

Just like your CCF, being aware of your own confirmation bias is the first step, and questioning yourself is the second.

Why is this so hard?

Because our stupid little brains want to be right *all of the time.*

Your brain wants to be right and wants to have the right answer. And when you're not used to questioning yourself or questioning your beliefs, but *really* used to not feeling good enough, your brain will automatically negate anything that doesn't line up with your most core beliefs. This looks like judgment and skepticism, like when I rolled my eyes at journaling and meditation and now I have an obnoxiously long morning routine that incorporates both.

So yes - even if the thing you think you're right about is the fact that you're a stupid, worthless piece of shit, your brain will be hellbent on continuing to believe so. You are *so* used to believing that you're not good enough, or capable enough, or smart enough, that any information to the contrary is vehemently rejected as *wrong.*

But what if *you* were wrong? One of my mentors, Dielle Charon, posed this question to me and the other women in her mastermind of multiple 6-figure earners. It blew our minds.

What if everything you think you know and believe can be perceived and understood completely differently than how you're taking it?

This is why most people who are on a spiritual or personal development journey feel lost, confused, more emotional than they're used to, and generally at war with themselves.

They are experiencing an inner conflict of what they think they know and believe, and the possibility that all of it is fucking *wrong*.

What if this entire time, you've been wrong about how worthy you really are? What if all of your "I'm not good enough" thoughts and feelings are just *programs* your brain has been running for years and years? Shortcuts that your brain takes whenever you do something new, or mess up, or something comes into your awareness that you want to have or do or achieve? What if it was just a pre-programmed response? And what if that pre-programmed response could be changed?

And so the journey *actually* begins, here, in the messy parts of your big, beautiful, stupid brain.

Your Inner Imposter

Let's start off with the basics - it's not you criticizing you inside your head. It's your inner imposter.

Your inner imposter is interchangeable with your inner critic. It is the voice in your head that you believe to be you. It is the voice that questions your capabilities, says you can't do things, holds you back from taking action, thinks perfectionism is a good thing, and says things to you that you would never, in your right mind, say to someone you love.

Your inner imposter might be one voice, or it might be several. I have a client whose inner imposter sounds like her mother. I have another client whose inner imposter sounds like several people from her old workplace.

It doesn't matter what the voice sounds like; you just need to know that there's always two of you in your head: your true self and your inner imposter.

They are not the same. The voice that tells you you're not good enough is not the same one that motivates you.

Up until this point, you may have believed that you *need* to change your self-talk because you're mean as fuck to yourself.

But what if it's not you talking? What if it is every failure, every mistake, every asshole in your life talking? What if it was the frenemy on the playground who was jealous of you talking? What if it was the boss who didn't think boundaries existed talking?

I cannot stress this enough - your inner imposter is **not you.**

They are just a pattern of thinking you are used to having. Patterns of thinking that can be interrupted, changed, worked through, molded, released, and transformed.

Name them. No, literally, give them a name. I named mine Rhonda. And whenever a thought comes up that is unkind, shaming, unpleasant, uncalled for, something that you'd never ever say to your best friend... name it for what it is - your inner imposter trying something.

"Okay, but once I'm done cussing that bitch out, what do I *do* to actually change my thoughts?"

Your Thoughts are a Dialogue, Not a Ted Talk

So you know how we talked about incongruency with our thoughts and feelings?

In your big, beautiful, stupid, messy brain - you are experiencing an inner conflict of "I'm not good enough" and "I AM good enough."

You feel good enough on the weeks where you got great feedback from your boss or a client.

You don't feel good enough when you have an uncomfortable meeting with the rigid CEO or when someone says they don't want to work with you after a sales call.

You feel good enough when you're having fun with your friends.

You don't feel good enough when one of them appears mad at you, and you wonder if you did something wrong.

It is a constant game of back and forth in your brain, and

the brain loves certainty, remember? So it's doing mental gymnastics trying to figure out which one is true.

This is where the cognitive dissonance comes into play again - you're holding two conflicting ideas at once. And because our brains are hardwired to predict danger, which used to be things that could kill us but are now things that just hurt our feelings, like rejection, failure, judgment, criticism, ostracism *(which to be honest, we really do believe those feelings can kill us...)* it makes sense that your brain wants to focus on the negative.

That's why the good thoughts and feelings feel much more fleeting than the negative ones. That's why your brain creates a blindspot where your accomplishments and accolades used to be when you feel like shit. That's why, when you ARE feeling good and confident for longer than normal, your brain decides to tell you that the other shoe is going to drop and inevitably, something bad will happen.

It's good news you have times where you feel good enough, right? Absolutely, and what we always want to do is strengthen that muscle of feeling into your enoughness, so you come back to it more often than you fall into "not enough" land.

Truthfully, you will always be overcoming imposter syndrome, because it will come up in different ways and at different levels, especially when you're going after the things you want. And each time, you get stronger and stronger as your internal programming begins to shift, and your brain begins to expand its capacity to hold your worthiness even more, each and every time.

This is having a foundation of worthiness. It is not free of suffering or pain or negativity - but it is being resilient to it.

And that all begins with your thoughts. Those negative thoughts that are essentially around the topic of you not feeling good enough.

Instead of trying to do something huge and will take a while, like reprogramming all of your beliefs since birth - let's start small. I want you to learn to *choose* your second thought.

Not your first. Your second.

Because your thoughts are a dialogue, but you're treating them like a never-ending Ted Talk.

You are in conversation with yourself, all day. Sometimes it's you and you. Sometimes it's you and your inner imposter. Regardless, you are having a myriad of thoughts at once, and if you look at them as a conversation, it means you are open to dialoguing with them instead of deciding that every thought you're having is a real and true fact.

So, if you have the thought of "I never know what I'm doing", the goal wouldn't be to change that thought and berate yourself for having it.

Your goal would be to dialogue with yourself - and consciously choose the second thought.

Over time, you will begin to rewire your neural pathways and change your internal programming, to where your first thought is not so negative or degrading. You may even get to a point where your first thought is "I'm a bad ass bitch and I can do anything."

Baby steps though, okay? One of my favourite ways to explain the process of changing your thoughts is with skiing.

Imagine that you're at the top of the hill, and you have two options - the bunny hill, or the black diamond. You've been skiing for a while, but you're not quite a pro yet. The bunny hill is grooved and smooth - you've been over it a million times before. You're familiar with it, you know where all the turns are; it's your comfort zone. You know what to expect.

The bunny hill is the path of least resistance for your brain. It is composed of all of the negative thoughts and programming that is so automatic and subconscious to you, that sometimes you don't even realize that you're on the path *(like when you drive home from work and disassociate, ending up in your driveway)*.

But then, there's the black diamond. This path represents thinking different thoughts, ones that are empowering and motivating and are conducive to your personal growth. You've barely spent any time there, and when you do, it feels uncomfortable and uncertain. You're not completely sold on it. It doesn't feel safe. The black diamond isn't grooved as smoothly as the bunny hill is. It's unfamiliar to you.

My parents took us skiing for the first time in Alberta, Canada when I was 12. The lessons were all booked up for the first half of the day, so they literally took me to the top of the mountain and said, "Let's go"! I do not recommend *(I still remember the bruises and almost crashing into a tree and my Dad yelling "PIZZZZAAA" at me while I catapulted down the hill)*.

Anyways, what I want **you** to do is continuously say fuck the bunny hill, I'm ready to make the black diamond my new normal.

Here's the thing - you *will* end up back on the bunny hill. It's inevitable. You'll be uncomfortable, uncertain of where you're going, and maybe you'll feel lost. So you'll find yourself, sometimes automatically, back on the bunny hill of "I'm not good enough, it's not working" etc.

But that's okay, as long as you *recognize* you're on the bunny hill, and then get your ass back on the black diamond.

Your brain is literally programmed to take the bunny hill. The easy route. The one you're familiar with. It's wired to keep you safe from danger, like an animal wanting to eat you. But now, since most of us are not in physical danger on a daily basis, you're afraid of other things, like feeling uncomfortable, fear of rejection, and possible threats to your character or inner sense of safety & certainty.

It doesn't matter if you spent the whole day on the black diamond and then you wiped out at the bottom and had to take the bunny hill for your last run.

It doesn't matter if you hit a snag on the black diamond and had to climb your way out of some deep powder.

Just keep making the conscious choice to choose differently. Observe the first thought, and choose the second thought.

So, Jill, your first piece of expert advice is to just talk to myself in a nicer way? Florals for spring? Groundbreaking. But seriously, let me tell you why *no one else* is teaching you how to overcome imposter syndrome in this way... because of a Master's degree I dutifully obtained because I thought I *should,* and then worried that it was completely useless - until right this second!

Through completing my Master's degree in Conflict Analysis and Management from Royal Roads University *(home of the X-Men castle, which is a much more interesting fact than the degree itself)* I came to find that conflict among parties is usually resolved through interests-based dialoguing and empathy.

"Interests-based" means that there is a reason why people do what they do and say what they say. They are usually acting from their own experiences, and are in conflict because they believe that their own interests are at stake. To effectively resolve conflict, we need to understand where the other person is coming from and open the floor to discussion, and if parties are in relationship with one another and want to move forward productively in that relationship, they must have empathy, compassion, and understanding for the other parties' interests.

So listen up, bitch - the reason why you're reading this and why you're on this stupid personal development journey is because you want to believe in yourself and feel worthy. Love yourself may be too strong right now, but at the very least, you want to *like* yourself.... Right? Right????

Here's the truth - people that believe in themselves, *love* themselves. They look at themselves with compassion, not judgment or criticism. They speak to themselves kindly. They aim to look at their reasons for doing things, past regrets, and past decisions with empathy and compassion for their former selves. They are in *relationship* with themselves, instead of at war with themselves.

Because they want to be happy. And they know that happiness is not all about their external world. It's how they feel about themselves on a daily basis. And being kind to yourself, having emotional resilience to tough out the hard shit in life, and learning to live in the present moment is what happiness truly is.

These people are not unicorns living in my magical forest - I swear, they're real. They are people who have done the work. They are people who have learned from their mistakes but didn't shame themselves for their mistakes. They are people who are in dialogue with themselves and don't make their emotions mean anything about them, even when they have hard days. They are all people who have grappled with their path to true worthiness. *They haven't always been this way, they've had to work at it - and continue to, everyday.*

Very early on in my coaching career, I went live on Instagram to talk about compound interest. No, I didn't become a finance bro overnight; I talked about how all of the work you do on yourself consistently, over a period of time, builds on each other. It all adds up, compounding on top of your already-present results, and you get to keep those results, forever, and keep adding to the pile.

So while today, you might do a meditation and only feel a teensy bit better - if you do it every day, in a couple of months maybe you yell at someone in traffic and then lean back and chuckle at your outburst of anger, observing it instead of continuing to be angry. Or maybe you catch a negative thought and immediately counter it with something empowering. Or maybe you pass judgment about someone and realize that it's coming from a belief system that you unconsciously subscribed to, but no longer fits with how you *want* to see the world.

Changing your thoughts is a process. In a world of quick wins, impatience, incessant dopamine hits through social media validation, and the "I want it now" mentality that so many of us have adopted...you can take your time. You don't have to be perfect today; actually, it's guaranteed you will never be perfect. But if you keep working at it, you will undoubtedly feel better, believe in yourself more, and maybe, MAYBE.... even love yourself.

shudders in self-deprecation

Seriously, what are we even doing on this floating rock, headed towards certain death, if we are not enjoying our lives, bettering ourselves, and speaking to ourselves with the kindness that we afford to everyone else *but* ourselves?

There is quite literally no other alternative. If you want to be miserable, if you want to believe the world is against you, if you want to take zero responsibility for your own life and your own happiness, if you want to continue chasing things and experiences that you think will make you happy when you'll still have the same miserable thoughts during said thing *(like when you tell yourself you can't wait for vacation to fully relax and then you absolutely don't)*....then you can choose that.

You have to be in it for the long haul. You have to decide that you're worth it, and that no experience or setback or negative thought will derail your progress. Because again, what's the alternative? What if, by taking responsibility for changing your thoughts, your relationships get 10x better? You released shame and guilt from something that happened in your past? You didn't think your mental illness or your mistakes define you?

What if all of that, and so much more, was possible, just by changing your internal dialogue?

It is. And it starts with your thoughts.

Journaling Exercise - Inner Imposter vs. Highest Self

1. Brain dump your current thoughts into your journal for 5 minutes.

2. Pick out the thoughts that you want to work on/change.

3. Start by taking each thought, writing it out, and then under it, *responding* to the thought with how

your highest self would want to think, feel, and move forward from that thought.

Head to www.jillianparekh.com/yns-book to see an example of this exercise.

How to Stop Overthinking

Next time your brain is going a hundred miles a minute, stop yourself and think, "What do I want my next thought to be?"

Imagine the inside of a machine where gears are constantly turning, and imagine all of them slowly coming to a stop. When you bring attention to the thoughts you're thinking, you become the observer of your thoughts instead of just the thinker of your thoughts.

Doing this is powerful work. For one, you will realize that you can actually slow down your thoughts enough to observe them.

And secondly, you will realize that every thought you have can truly be optional. You can choose to think whatever you want, and most of your thoughts up until this point have been the product of uninvestigated beliefs.

You may not be able to catch *all* of your thoughts, because we have thousands of them a day. But the ones that are on an unending loop, especially the ones around what you're capable of, what you can achieve, your worthiness, the success you think you'll "never" have...these thoughts are not true, you have just thought them for a very long time, on repeat, and have never questioned them or even wondered if they could be untrue.

But what if you slowed down your mind enough to ask yourself, "What do I want my next thought to be?"

And then, on purpose, you chose your next thought?

The Song of Your People AKA The Stupid Fucking Beliefs You Picked Up From Your Lineage

You are made up of everything and everyone from your lineage, whether you know it or not.

You are also made up of everything from the environments in which you grew up.

You have beliefs, ideas, thoughts, opinions, and stories about yourself, the world, how it works, money, and just about everything else, that have all been passed down onto you.

There was a time where you were unconsciously adopting those beliefs, but now, you are becoming aware of the fact that they are just that - beliefs.

You can love your family, without subscribing to their way of thinking.

You can honour your lineage, without following in their footsteps.

The only reason why you believe it needs to be done the way they've always done it, is because you have never opened your mind up to there being a different way.

What you can keep: Thoughts that are helpful to you. Beliefs that feel good.

What you can throw away: Literally everything else.

This may feel impossible at first, especially if you still spend a lot of time with your family. Beliefs about the world and other people, ways of thinking, and patterns of behaviour may *feel* like they are the only option for you and your life...

But there are so many different ways to think and to be. The only reason why you're subscribing to *this* way of thinking and being is because it's what you've always known. And it's comfortable and safe and predictable to continue believing what you've always believed.

Again, what might be happening as you open up your mind to the fact that you *don't* need to live the same life as your parents *(even though there's nothing wrong with that)* or that you *don't* need to work your ass off to make money in this day and age, is that ole cognitive dissonance. Because while your beliefs have always been one way, once you start opening yourself up to the possibility of different belief systems, you may feel a little wonky and unsettled, wondering what is true.

Whatever you decide to be true for you is what will show up in your external reality, if that's what you focus on.

Think about your life and where it's gone or where it's headed, depending on how old you are. Was this consciously created by you and your decisions? Or, when you think about it, did you unconsciously take a path that someone else in your family took?

This isn't to shame you for the way you've made decisions, but instead an opportunity for you to look at what decisions you *have* made, and if they've been intentional or unintentional.

Your life is yours. Your decisions are yours. Maybe the reason why you don't feel like yourself and you feel like a fraud is because you've unconsciously adopted an identity that is not aligned with what *you* truly want. A big part of imposter syndrome is truly not knowing who you are, what you like, and what you desire, for fear of it being wrong or bad or for fear of not being able to have it.

But if the slate was wiped clean, and your wants, needs, and desires were valid - what would you do? If the slate was wiped clean of the unhelpful thought patterns and belief systems from your family of origin and the environment in which you were raised... What would be possible?

One way I shift my beliefs is with EFT Tapping.

EFT stands for Emotional Freedom Techniques[6], and can be described as psychological acupuncture. It is the practice of tapping on the energetic meridian points of your body, focusing on what you want to release and then focusing on what you want to embody. As a Master EFT Practitioner, EFT Tapping has helped me and my coaching clients completely rewire our neural pathways in order to release old beliefs and stories and step into who we want to be.

Here's an "Introduction to EFT" video I recorded to get you started.

---

[6] *Thought Field Therapy and its derivatives: Rapid relief of mental health problems through tapping on the body, by Phil Mollon, 2007*

And then here's a tapping I made for you, "Feeling Worthy & Good Enough for your Desires".

You can find these resources at www.jillianparekh.com/yns-book and you can find more EFT tapping videos on my YouTube channel "Jillian Parekh Coaching".

You're Not Too Sensitive, Bitch

Most people do not like being told that they are responsible for their happiness. That's because most people are hypocrites, neck-deep in the suppression of their experiences but reactive to those who match their energy. It's okay for *them* to discount their experiences, bypass their emotions, and numb themselves to the pain they've endured - but if someone else were to, they'd throw hands.

So even though I basically yelled at you in the first couple of chapters, I'm going to coddle you for a tiny, tiny bit. But then it's back to calling you a lil bitch.

Your trauma is valid - micro or macro.

Your experiences are valid.

The way you feel is valid.

Being a victim of racism, sexism, homophobia... It is all real and valid.

The way someone made you feel is valid.

It was wrong what happened to you.

It wasn't fair.

It shouldn't have happened.

You did not deserve it.

You are not less than because of it.

You are not less than because of your mental illness or because of the house you grew up in.

It doesn't mean anything about you - but it *does* matter.

Don't discount your experiences as non-traumatic or "not as bad", either. When we discredit our experience and feel like we're not "allowed" to be upset or affected by something, all it does is make us hold onto the feelings from that experience *more*, with an added layer of shame attached to it.

Just *thinking* about everything you've gone through is not enough. It needs to be acknowledged and validated - whether it's through social support like family, friends, a therapist, in your journal, or with a coach.

If you don't do this, it will continue to block you, create resistance, and will only continue your cycle of internal justification - which is where you'll continue feeling righteous, bitter, and will stay in victimhood, believing that you're the way you are because of these things, and you're not responsible for getting yourself out of it.

Think of your brain like your attic. You have holiday decorations, childhood memories, and all of the random shit that you don't really think about until you go up there and see it all.

Some of it *really* needs to be cleared out. It's just taking up space and collecting dust in the corner, when you could put something more important there, or just even create space for something new to come along.

If you don't clear up unnecessary baggage from your brain and just try to pretend like it doesn't exist, you might accidentally and unexpectedly run into it when you're trying to do something else and hurt yourself. You might see it, your body will feel like you're back in time, and all the residual feelings you didn't deal with will come up and mess up your day. Trauma, big T or little t, is anchored into the body through experiences where we felt an intense emotion.

The fact of the matter is - the past exists only in our mind. It used to be our present; but now, the only way it exists is as a memory in your mind and a feeling in your body. You get to decide what to do with it.

Everything that happened to you that is affecting you to this day is completely valid.

It is a reason, but not an excuse. Don't confuse the two.

Remember - we are all hypocrites. You aren't the victim in every single story you have, and you consciously know you're responsible for some things; however, as we already know, the brain can hold several conflicting ideas at once. You may feel responsible for one thing, but only because of that other thing that you weren't responsible for.

My client had someone close to them experience depression in their early 20s, and a lot of things went wrong as a result. For a long time, they numbed out, bypassed their feelings, and didn't address their mental health; but if they were asked about moving forward or doing better, they'd blame everything on being depressed and would become upset with the person trying to talk to them. Internally, their self-talk was deprecating, negative, and self-sabotaging. The reason why this person was depressed wasn't their fault whatsoever - but the following events where their actions determined their outcomes were their responsibility, and the shame from those mistakes made things even worse.

So while you can't evade responsibility for things you have caused yourself... this is where self-forgiveness comes in.

For what's happened to you, been done to you, intentionally or unintentionally - **acknowledgement, validation, and empathy for yourself - and if appropriate, an attempt at understanding why the other parties' did what they did.**

For what you've done because of what's been done to you, intentionally or unintentionally - **self-compassion and self-forgiveness.**

These things are what moves you fluidly from awareness to personal responsibility.

Because here's the thing - awareness without taking action is *evading* personal responsibility. It is a sign of low emotional intelligence, and yes, I did just low-key call emotionally immature people dumbasses. You can be the most self-aware person in the world and understand why you are the way you are, but if it's causing you *(or anybody else in your life that you love, for that matter)* undue pain or hardship, it's time to put that awareness into action.

But this is only when you have had *your* pain validated. Because if you don't do that first, taking responsibility will feel a lot like shame.

My business coach gave me some tough love at the end of

2021 when I was trying to figure out why I wasn't getting the results that I wanted. I was being extremely hard on myself, and she kept asking me to take responsibility for my results. I was extremely reactive and felt frustrated and emotional for days - because for me, I had only ever learned that taking responsibility meant feeling shameful about how I got to where I was in the first place.

Think about the correlation between the word "responsibility" and your own, unique experiences. You will probably associate responsibility with things that aren't so fun, like paying bills, being accountable, doing the *right* thing, being who others expect you to be...

We go deeper into shame in a different chapter. But I want you to acknowledge that there might be a piece of you, as well, that associates responsibility with shame.

You're afraid that if you start being responsible for things in your life, they could go badly. They could go wrong. You might still not get what you want. You might realize you're *actually* a failure, and then you'll have no one to blame but yourself.

That shit hurts. But you're more resilient than you think you are. You have made it through every shitty fucking thing that has happened to you. You're a little bruised, a little beat up, and your thoughts kind of suck. But we're working on it.

The past and what's been done to you, your sadness, your anger, your frustration, your desperation, your unworthiness - they can all exist at the same time, remember? You are allowed to be upset about something that hurt you, but you can also take responsibility for how you responded to it.

One of my very first clients in 2018 completely ghosted me

after three sessions. I had no idea what I did wrong, and because I felt completely incapable and not good enough, I spun out about it. I incessantly emailed her, messaged her, and tried to get into contact with her. I emotionally responded to her rejection by telling her she was rude and disrespectful.

She was wrong. But so was I, acting from my hurt instead of processing it and understanding what I was making it mean.

You're not too sensitive, bitch. You're *reactive* because you're holding onto pain and trauma and heavy shit that you think is better left unsaid, until you get into a fight with someone and all of that hurt and anger spills out in a way you're not exactly proud of. Or until you get rejected by a potential client and you feel like a kid on the playground who's been excluded.

It is safe to acknowledge the hurt that others have caused you without needing to text them about it.

It is safe to acknowledge what you've done wrong without standing in the middle of Walmart and reading an entry out of your journal.

It is safe to be everything imperfect, messy, and fucked up.

And none of it means anything about where you can go from here.

Hold a hand over your heart, and repeat after me:

"I choose to see all of my past experiences with empathy, compassion, and love for my former self. I choose to relieve my brain from trying to figure out why things happened the way they did, or why they happened to me. I choose to stop making my past mean anything about where I'm headed or what I'm capable of. I choose to validate myself, and at the same time, take responsibility for my future self without shame or guilt. I choose to stay committed to this way of thinking, even if I fall off, even if I mess up, even if I start believing the stories my brain wants to tell me. I choose to have my own back, always".

Your path to self-acknowledgement and self-validation will not be a one-off. After this chapter, you can make a note for your coach or your therapist or you can brain dump in your journal. And, expect for other things from your past to come up randomly and sporadically, where you'll have to come back to this practice of acknowledging and validating your experience, and choosing to move forward from that. As you begin to change your thoughts and beliefs, the reason *why* you have those thoughts and beliefs will become apparent and this is when the acknowledgement comes in.

Let me give you an example:

If I'm wanting to change a belief about money, such as "There's never enough for me", chances are that my brain will bring up experiences, like when my brother was sent to Wales for a school rugby tournament, and my parents told me that because they sent him there, they couldn't send me to Venezuela with my best friend. My brain will bring up this experience as evidence.

I can acknowledge and validate what I made this mean - I'm not as important. There's not enough for me. I don't deserve it. I'm not good enough. I wasn't chosen.

I can acknowledge and validate that it was unfair for *me* and that it made *me* feel bad. I can also understand that my parents did so much for me and continue to, even in adulthood. My parents took us all on vacations and trips and I always had what I needed and wanted. My parents love me just as much as they love my brother *(I mean, jury's still out on that one because he's the only boy and the oldest).*

And I can take responsibility for this now, deciding that little Jilly had no way of emotionally regulating herself and she struggled with her confidence, so she turned this into a story that she is still clinging to in order to support her bullshit story of "I'm not good enough".

And I can choose differently.

Your process won't always be so cut and dry as this example. But at the root of it - you *want* to love yourself, and that starts with compassion and empathy. It turns into acknowledgement and validation, because a lot of the time we never get that from other people, especially those who have hurt us. And then, we can decide that this story won't hold us back anymore.

What will you decide?

The Forgiveness Meditation

Go to www.jillianparekh.com/yns-book and download The Forgiveness Meditation.

REFRAMING THE PAST DOESN'T MEAN CHANGING IT

In that example with my parents, I chose to see the situation differently than how my 16-year-old self saw it. **The way we experience something is not always the truth**. This does not mean that our feelings aren't valid - we are always allowed to feel how we feel. But by going back and assessing an experience from a different perspective, especially when at the time our recanting of the event may be affected by age, life experience, and the inability to see through another's eyes - we can reframe the situation to help us in the future, rather than looking back and feeling the sting of the memory.

As a side note: this is not appropriate in the event where you are a victim of abuse, severe trauma, racism, and other experiences of oppression. Nothing that happened to you is okay, and you didn't deserve it. And in no way am I giving leeway or acceptance to the person or people who have caused your pain.

As I said in the beginning of the chapter - your trauma is valid.

You are allowed to be angry, hurt, and you are allowed to say "Fuck that person/people/situation/experience" for the rest of your life.

Reframing the past and allowing yourself to heal from hurt you have endured AND hurt you have caused is for *you,* and *you only.*

It is only for your gain, not for your loss.

We cannot change the past, but we can decide to see it differently, if that's what helps.

We cannot change the past, but we can cry and break down, and then pick ourselves back up, if that's what helps.

We cannot change the past, but we can decide to do whatever we need to do to move forward, if that's what helps.

Change your perspective from sitting in the story to walking towards the outcome.

What does your highest self want to feel about this?

What does your highest self want to make this mean about you?

What will help you get to a peaceful place and an abundant life?

You get to choose how to think about something and how it affects you in the future.

Everything You Do is to Avoid a Feeling

That's it, that's the tweet.

Everything you do is to avoid a feeling. And this is because you're afraid about what the repercussions will be from feeling that feeling.

If you're afraid to take a job interview, you're probably afraid that you won't get the job and it'll feel like a knife to the heart, and then you'll spiral into shame and lay on your couch for six weeks.

If you're afraid to show up on live video on Instagram, you're afraid you won't get the views or engagement to validate you, and then you'll feel embarrassed and never go live again.

If you're afraid to say something that's been on your mind that you know a lot of people you love don't agree with, you're afraid they'll be mad at you or judge you, and then you'll question your opinions and thoughts or think you're stupid.

You're afraid to feel something negative, *especially* if you have past evidence of self-sabotaging behaviour as a result of it.

For example - I have ADHD and have emotional dysregulation issues as a result. I either feel ALL my fucking feelings at once or I suppress them. In 2020, my childhood home burnt down. My parents still lived there with their dog, Lucy, our 15-year-old cat, Monty, and my sister had moved back in because of the pandemic. Everyone survived except for our Monty man, which was devastating, and the house was not salvageable by any means. Some of our photo albums were saved, but mostly everything was gone. It was something you're always afraid of happening, and it happened to us. My sister had to move in with me and my fiancé for seven months, and I was working full-time and running my busy online coaching business on the side.

I gained about 25 lbs because of the pandemic, undiagnosed ADHD and seeking dopamine from food, and eating my feelings every night instead of feeling them - because a girl had shit to do. I had a business to run, bills to pay, a full-time job to clock into, clients that needed me - and that meant that I (subconsciously) suppressed my feelings so I could survive.

Thus, when I began to unwind this pattern, I realized that I would overeat if things were difficult emotionally - and it caused me to be very anxious about bad things happening and feeling emotional, because then I would overeat again.

We have all had a moment (or several) where we recognized that feeling shitty was in fact, shitty. And maybe it affected a job or affected a relationship or affected our character. Maybe your boyfriend broke your heart and you swore you'd never open yourself up to love again, because it hurt so bad that you ended up drunk on a Tuesday when you had a 9:00 a.m. meeting the next day, which you slept through, and now you have terrible hang-xiety. Your brain associates the pain of the heartbreak to the self-sabotaging behavior, so it subconsciously says to you, "Nope, we no love again. Too dangerous when mixed with uncertainty and tequila.".

And thus, we learned that it is better to become resilient to our feelings, instead of *actually* feeling them. We learn that there are only two options: have our emotions bounce off of us like rubber or absorb them and sit in them like water. The latter always seem worse, and that's because very few of us have been taught that **we don't have to make our emotions mean anything.**

To numb out or ignore our emotions is actually *not* resiliency at all; it's self-inflicted oppression.

So let's tackle that first bit - **your emotions don't have to mean anything.** They are just feelings in your body, stagnant energy that needs to be moved and processed. It takes 90 seconds for an emotion to move through your body[7] *(if you allow it instead of resisting it)*. Emotions come from your thoughts - and here's the thing, most of the time, that thought is subconscious. Meaning, it flies under your awareness radar and immediately evokes an emotional response before you can even identify what the thought was.

Dr. Joe Dispenza talks about the body and the mind working in tandem with each other in a programmed system in which he calls your "emotional quota"[8]. We all have one, and it is the state that your body is most comfortable being in. Because our thoughts create our feelings, we are used to having the same kind of thoughts, which evoke the same kinds of feelings, which then influence our beliefs and behaviors. And because

[7] *90 Seconds to Emotional Resilience by Dr. Alyson M. Stone, 2019*
[8] *Breaking the Habit of Being Yourself by Dr. Joe Dispenza, 2013*

the brain is like a computer, we log these programs (or ways of being and existing) and the brain uses these programs as shortcuts for our lives, activating the programs so our responses to stimuli are more immediate because the brain is lazy and wants to take the path of least resistance.

Just like the ski hill analogy, your body is used to feeling a certain way in accordance with your thoughts. Your body is used to feeling anxiety, fear, worthlessness, desperation, and etc. So when you start trying to change your thoughts to those of empowerment and self-compassion, your body ain't gonna be on board. It's going to resist it. It's going to be like hmmmm, we don't believe that new thought, because it doesn't help us get back to the normal states we're used to - which is feeling anxious and shitty. Let's go back to the thoughts we KNOW are true, because that fulfills our emotional quota.

So, all of this being said, can you get on board with the fact that your shitty emotions are just that - shitty emotions? You're going to need this as you begin to change the dialogue in your head. Your brain is working against you by already having so many ingrained reactions to the things in your life, like when someone won't let you merge onto the highway *(can you tell I have road rage???)*. It's going to feel uncomfortable and you're going to hit up against resistance. Your feelings and your thoughts won't always match, and you'll have to work at getting them on board with each other.

But remember what I said about conflicting thoughts, beliefs, and emotions - it's okay. It's normal. You're not doing anything wrong.

Speak to yourself this way when you have a big feeling. If you feel angry, sad, anxious, fearful, lonely - sit with it for a second. Notice where it's located in the body. Allow it to be felt, without attaching yourself to the thoughts your brain is throwing at you, like "We shouldn't be feeling this, it's because that guy flipped me off, I'm so stupid, why can't I get it right, why did they mess up my Starbucks order" - breathe, and imagine your thoughts are like clouds in the sky. You don't need to comment on them or latch onto them. Just allow them to pass.

We are not trying to change the fact that you *have* emotions. Of course you do, and you always will. We are trying to change your resistance and discomfort to *having* emotions. Instead of changing the emotion, we aim to interrupt the self-sabotaging pattern that occurs when you are trying to remedy the negative emotion and when you're trying to make it mean everything about you and your life and your future.

For example, I experience symptoms of depression here and there, and with that depression comes bouts of sadness. People with ADHD also have emotional dysregulation issues, so we already don't handle our emotions well, and we have a tendency to hyperfixate on things, *including* emotions. So when I used to get sad or mad or whatever, I'd completely zero in on that emotion, think I was going to feel it forever, and start thinking about my entire life, everyone in it, my job, and etc., and make my emotions mean things were WRONG and needed to CHANGE.

I'd impulsively buy something I didn't need, another symptom of ADHD, for the dopamine fix. I'd pick a fight with my fiancé. I'd question my life's path. I'd want to change everything about my business at 1:00 a.m. And then, a couple of days later, I'd be on the up and up and laugh at how silly I was.

But these bouts of emotion that I made mean EVERYTHING

at the time they were happening *caused* self-sabotaging behaviors to happen, even if they were subtle. I went into credit card debt buying shit I didn't need. I'd take a perfectly fine situation with my fiancé and create conflict. I'd make change after change to my business, and then fear I'd appear inconsistent. Decisions I made in the height of my emotions had lasting effects even after the emotion inevitably subsided.

Your best course of action is to do what we call "riding the emotional wave"; experience the emotion, and do your best to feel it without attaching yourself to *any* thoughts you have as you're feeling the emotion.

This is so fucking hard. You will probably never get it perfect. Perfect doesn't exist, but *you* exist, a human feeling emotions like a human. When you're feeling a big emotion, your brain narrows its focus and fixates on what you're feeling so it can explain *why* you're feeling that way. This is also a biological response for your brain to hyperfocus on the problem, because it goes into hypervigilance mode to protect you. Ultimately, the brain just wants things to make sense, so it will try to make your emotions make sense, and then skip to resolution-mode, like when an emotionally immature parent can't handle their toddler having a tantrum.

When I am really in the thick of my emotional wave, I repeat to myself, "It is safe to have this emotion. Everything is okay." When I'm feeling really anxious, I sit there and allow the tightness in my chest to completely take over. It's extremely uncomfortable and I feel like I'm going to die, but then I usually bubble over in tears and I'm feeling better 15 - 20 minutes later. Before, my mind used to race about all the things I was anxious about, but now I'm way better at grounding myself and reminding myself that my thoughts aren't true, my brain is just trying to keep me safe, and at the end of the day, I am and always *will* be safe.

So, try it with me. Hand over your heart, and say, "It's safe to have this emotion. Everything is okay." You may feel a little anxious even saying that to yourself, because up until this point, you *didn't* feel safe feeling your emotions and thought they were something you needed to fix.

All of this being said - resistance to your emotions is *extremely* normal, and this may manifest as skepticality that you, in fact, do not need to feel your emotions. Or that you don't have a lot of them. Here's how your childhood/adolescence may have impacted that:

- No one held space for your emotions or told you it was okay to have them.

- You were expected to not have any big feelings, and when you did have them you were scolded, shamed, or even abused for "acting out".

- You were told to toughen up, and learned that any big feelings other than anger were a sign of weakness.

- You experienced a large amount of hardship and your brain repressed your emotions so you could protect yourself.

- Whenever you expressed yourself, someone was always trying to "fix" the problem you were having instead of letting you express yourself *(this is mostly done out of love and discomfort that others felt)*.

- You learned to associate being emotional or expressing yourself to being alone or excluded.

I could go on forever, but those are the big ones. And thus, as I stated throughout this chapter, whether you experienced one or all of these things...you have learned to make your big emotions *mean something bad*. Because the environment that you were raised in didn't or couldn't hold space for your big feelings, you subconsciously learned that it's because they meant something bad, and therefore, you must avoid them, or not feel them as much, or fix whatever problem you are having so you don't have them anymore.

But then, we grow up - and life gets inevitably harder, we have more responsibilities, and we deal with terrible things like illness, loss, unemployment, relationships and friendships ending, and etc.

And if we don't *know* that we can feel our feelings and not die, that we can feel our feelings and actually come out stronger... we will repress them. We will eat them. We will self-sabotage the good things. We will project our shame and guilt and fear onto others.

A feeling cannot destroy your life. But, a self-sabotaging action taken from resisting a feeling or making a feeling mean something it doesn't - that can fuck some shit up, for sure.

Up until I went to therapy in 2019, I didn't think I had anxiety. I just thought I stuttered and that I was embarrassed of my stutter, and therefore I was weak for always trying to avoid stuttering everywhere I went.

But whenever I had to go somewhere I was nervous about, I'd pick a fight with my fiancé, become extremely irritable or angry, or completely ruin my fun time by wishing I was anywhere else. I have a very distinct memory of being in the backseat of a car, and I was listening to a podcast where the host described anxiety as a tiny gray cloud over every part of their life. I immediately felt tears spring to my eyes - that is *exactly* how I felt, all of the time. It was then I decided to go to therapy, where she confirmed rather quickly that I presented as someone with anxiety. When I was diagnosed with generalized anxiety disorder and ADHD, I realized how much I had stuffed down my anxious feelings because they made me feel weak.

Becoming aware of my emotions, not making them mean anything, and letting them "bubble over" meant that I could express how I was feeling to my fiancé instead of picking a fight with him, use tools and mindset practices to process my emotions accordingly, and work through the racing thoughts instead of just deciding they were true and moving on to fix them immediately.

I wouldn't be able to do any of that if I kept on telling myself I wasn't supposed to be anxious or nervous or angry or whatever I had suppressed for so many years.

Again - it's not perfect. I still work on not making my emotions mean anything, not projecting onto those I love and who I'm certain won't abandon me, and not spiraling into believing all of my thoughts are true when I'm in the midst of my emotional wave. But the mere knowledge that I can feel my feelings and that they don't have to mean anything about who I am, where I'm going, and what I'm capable of? It makes moving through my emotional wave so much easier and way less painful.

If you take anything away from this chapter, I want you to know that you don't need to be afraid of your emotions. They can't kill you, it is safe to have them, and they don't mean anything about where you're going or what you'll do. Your brain will try and hijack your thoughts when you're in the midst of *your* emotional wave, but do your best to come back to the thought of "It's safe to have this emotion. Everything is okay."

Now listen, you might have *a lot* of repressed emotions. So, when you start allowing yourself to feel, more may come up than you realize. Hire a coach or go and see a therapist, invest in a journal, and allow yourself to process accordingly. It doesn't mean anything has gone wrong, it just means there was more under the surface than you realized. This isn't anything to be afraid of - it is incredibly healing to feel. It means you're alive.

Emotional Mirroring Exercise

Go to www.jillianparekh.com/yns-book and download the "Emotional Mirroring" exercise. This is for you to practice allowing your feelings to come up without making them mean anything, and letting them pass naturally.

Your resistance to feeling comes from the thought that it should not be happening. Which brings us to the next lesson...

"Should" is Just Shame with Sugar on Top

As a coach, I am a firm believer that in order to get to the light, we have to fumble through the darkness for a bit. Like when you're trying to find the light switch in your own damn house, and you bump into walls and other stationary things when you've quite literally lived there for years. Nevertheless, you fumble for the light switch after failing to see in the dark, and you try and try and try again until you finally get it.

We can't talk about overcoming imposter syndrome without talking about shame. Sorry Brené Brown, I'm coming for your brand. But here's the thing; shame never presents as shame, just like imposter syndrome doesn't always present as unworthiness.

Shame creeps in under the guise of "should". If you struggle with imposter syndrome, you have probably been "shoulding" all over yourself for as long as you can remember.

Should is the sugar on top of shame to make it more palatable.

We think thoughts that start with should, and suddenly we feel awful about ourselves. We tell ourselves stories about what we're supposed to know, where we're supposed to be in life, and how we're supposed to feel. All because your inner imposter's voice starts their sentences with, "You should…"

Should breeds shame by implying that you knew better, but disregarded that knowledge. When I made six figures for the first time in my life in 2020, and then promptly spent it all on business expenses and other things, I spent a good chunk of 2021 telling myself I shouldn't have done that. When in reality, money management at the 6-figure mark was not something I was familiar with. Being a person who had more than $3000/month was not something I was familiar with. Taxes, running a business, and investing for the future, were all things I knew nothing about. Yet, I beat myself up for months, feeling ashamed and stupid because my inner imposter kept proclaiming loudly that I should have known better, or I should have sought out the tools so I could do better.

"Should" is the inner imposter's go-to tactic. There's no arguing with should, especially if you believe that *you* are the voice of your inner imposter.

Something I teach my clients to do when they hear "should" in their head everyday is to rebuttal their inner imposter with "Where did I learn that?"

- Where did I learn that I should be married and own a house before turning 30?
- Where did I learn that I should file my taxes this way?
- Where did I learn that I shouldn't want to have a lot of money?
- Where did I learn that I should have known better in

- this situation?
- Where did I learn that I need to grow my business in this particular way?

When you ask yourself this question, the echo of someone else's voice will be heard. Or the memory of someone else's decision. Or you'll come up blank, because the brain is an asshole and will just *decide* that the "should" is valid, even if you don't know where it came from. But you can usually trace it back to a person or a past experience that taught you, whether directly or indirectly, unconsciously or consciously, how to be.

Here's a should for you: as you're overcoming imposter syndrome, "should" is something that *should be* flagged immediately. Whenever I hear a "should" cross my mind, I pay attention. The "should" is attempting to bang cymbals across my brain in order to distract me from shame slipping silently through the door.

Shame is enforced through the belief that there is a certain way to be, and it is not the way we are being. It is usually upheld by societal norms, religious restrictions, generational and familial belief systems, and/or cultural traditions. But when you struggle with a deep sense of unworthiness and imposter syndrome, shame can feel like just being embarrassed about who *you* are and what *you* do. Always feeling like you're doing something wrong, even if you're unsure about what the right way is.

This manifests by way of learning not to trust yourself and looking for external validation. Allowing yourself to think something or be something *only* when you see other people doing it, thinking it, or being it. Getting the validation that if other people are experiencing it, it's okay for you to experience it, too. This is a double-edged sword. On one hand, you realize (internally) that you're not alone. You exhale - alone, of course, because you would never dare share your shame. But on the other hand, you're left with the knowledge that you only decided to accept yourself because someone else was brave enough to speak it into the world.

Shame holds your self-acceptance hostage. It will repeatedly tell you that you are bad because of what you did or who you are, which will either keep you stuck in shame paralysis or you'll try to improve yourself on the premise of disliking yourself *(and in some cases, hating yourself)*.

Remember when I said that people who overcome imposter syndrome *love* themselves? Well, I hate to break it to you, but the whole point of improving yourself is to love and accept yourself more. It is extremely redundant to try to improve yourself from a place of "I suck, and I'm gonna try not to suck." This is usually from a place of feeling like you need to be something or do something in order to be worthy of being loved *by other people.* Newsflash - other people's versions of "enough" are not *your* version of enough. You will always be chasing validation and love if you *only* seek it from others and never learn to give it to yourself. Because if you don't give it to yourself, even if the love and acceptance from others is smacking you in the face, you won't recognize it, you won't count it, and you will continue to not feel good enough.

Let's take an example → Jackie is a stellar employee with a ton of imposter syndrome. She never feels good enough at work, despite the consistent praise she gets from her boss and the awards she gets for her performance. When she does feel good about herself, it's fleeting; but any wrong tone in an email or any tiny mistake she thinks she made - and she spirals, feeling like she's going to be reprimanded or fired. It doesn't matter how many times her boss tells her she's the shit, Jackie has a continuous stream of thoughts that she's not good enough, that she needs to do better, and that she can't make any mistakes or she'll be outed for not knowing what she's doing.

Jackie is not a bad person. She doesn't need to do anything external to prove that she is good enough; yet she feels like she is missing something and needs to be better. When really, the only things that need to change are her thoughts about herself, her own level of self-acceptance, and the tiptoeing around shame that she does. She is constantly waiting for the other shoe to drop externally, like for someone to say "Wow, you're not that good at your job", because that's what she actually thinks about herself. However, once she changes her internal lens and how *she* sees *herself,* she will undoubtedly feel better. And then yes, maybe she *will* perform better. Maybe her coworkers will notice she's less anxious and on-edge. Maybe she'll share a really cool, innovative idea that she was too afraid of sharing before. But she'll know on the inside that she's a good person and that she's doing her best, *without* anything external to her actually changing.

The bottom line is that shame is just another shitty thing that lies under imposter syndrome, because we think it's only a matter of time until we're revealed as bad. And then it bullies us into silence. Imposter syndrome affects over 70% of people[9] in their lifetime, yet many workplaces don't address it whatsoever. Barely anyone in the online entrepreneurial space was seriously talking about it when I decided to specialize in it. If everybody fucking feels this way, why is no one talking about it?!

Because we're afraid that if we reveal that we *feel* like we don't

---

[9] *The Imposter Phenomenon, International Journal of Behavioral Science,* 2011

know what we're doing, we may actually find out that we don't know what we're doing. So to minimize the risk of judgment or rejection, we keep it inside. And because we don't work through it or talk about it, we just assume that it's true.

It's time for you to air out the shame under your imposter syndrome.

1. You're going to catch your thoughts when you start one with "I should". Should will sneak past you more often than not, so it is a process to become accustomed to catching it over time. Whenever you catch a "should" thought, question yourself: Where did this come from? Who told me that? Where did I learn that? Is this really what I *should* be doing? Is it going to produce the outcome of a happier, more fulfilled life?

Don't take this literally. I don't mean for you to question yourself if you think, "Should I eat a meatball sub or a panzerotti for lunch today?" Question yourself when you're making decisions about your life, your career, and your relationships. Question yourself when you're feeling shitty and when "should" keeps coming up to distract you from the oh-so-familiar shame trying to seep into your thoughts.

2. I want you to *really* think about what you're afraid of people knowing about you. What are you afraid someone will find out if they truly knew you? What are you afraid of someone saying if you made a mistake? This is called "shadow work" in spiritual circles, where you examine your fears & triggers in a safe space in order for you to heal them. So, again - hire a coach, go to a therapist, or invest in a journal. Give yourself space to answer these questions:

If people really knew me, they would think...

What am I afraid of someone thinking about me?

What am I making it mean if I don't live up to my potential?

If someone wanted to really hurt me, they would say I was
_____

Exploring your answers to these questions will take time. It's so, so important for you to know that you are good enough and loved and worthy and that all of the things you think about yourself aren't true. You are not bad. You are just *afraid* that you're bad, or wrong, or whatever else that makes you hide your true self in the shadows *(pun intended)*.

This isn't the end of shame. A lot of people were parented by way of shame, use it to motivate themselves, and truly believe that shame can be helpful. But let me ask you this - is anything that makes you think you're a bad person just for *existing* something worth holding onto?

Start dialoguing with yourself when shame tries to slip inside while a girl guide named Should stands at the door. Think of them like estranged family members - they used to attend holiday functions, but you grew up and realized how detrimental those relationships were to your life. Now they are just memories, and are unwelcome in your new home of self-acceptance and worthiness.

Disappointment is A (Shitty) Part of Life

If "should" carries the obnoxious cymbals so shame can slink in discreetly, disappointment is the encore.

Disappointment is the encore; because as a high-achieving woman who has learned to dialogue with her brain and banish "should" to the grave, disappointment can come swooping in and present itself as useful to your life. **Disappointment is the unwelcomed aftermath of an unmet expectation.** It is the evidence of a desire, a wish, a goal that was unfulfilled - and when you feel like a fraud, you will usually attribute it to yourself as being the reason for the disappointment. Or, you might just go straight to regarding *yourself* as The Disappointment.

Because if you knew better, if you did know what you were talking about, if you were knowledgeable and capable and everything else that you're trying to prove you are...you'd achieve your goals. You'd feel good about yourself. You wouldn't make mistakes. You'd have what you want.

But the difference between shame and disappointment is that shame doesn't deserve your time. How you work through shame is verbalizing it, bringing it into the light, and watching it melt like the Wicked Witch of the West. Disappointment, on the other hand, needs to be felt in order to have everything you've ever wanted.

It also needs to be felt so it can be unlinked to shame. It is only the fear of disappointment turning to shame that keeps us from wanting to feel disappointed. We're afraid that if we don't achieve a goal that we make in a bullshit timeline that we set for ourselves, we'll be disappointed in ourselves, and then we'll feel ashamed - which is the most desolate, harshest thing you can feel. And then you'll self-sabotage and spiral even further into self-loathing.

Disappointment needs to be felt so we can learn how to make it no big deal. It's only fatal to your dreams if you decide that being disappointed is the end, instead of deciding that you can keep going, take a new route, and discover a different way.

Shame is something that is unnecessary to feel. This doesn't mean you'll never feel it - you probably will, a lot.

But, there will come a time where you realize that shame is unnecessary because it doesn't serve a function. Shame says "You are bad", and it's kind of like arguing with an angry Karen at the grocery store - unnecessary, volatile, and neither of you want what's best for each other. It is not a requirement of life to feel shame, and it doesn't serve you to hang around it, thinking it's serving a purpose. Heal it, yes - but don't hang out with it.

Disappointment swoops in as shame's last ditch effort to fuck you up; but unlike shame, I think feeling it is necessary. Because if you don't feel it, you will avoid it and be afraid of it, which will only cause more pain & self-sabotage.

After making six figures for two years in a row, I was on the couch with my fiancé and asked him to help me pay my portion of our rent. I had a successful business on the outside, but on the outside, my money management skills were still being nurtured, and I still had credit card debt that was taking a lot of my extra cash. Because of this, my sales had dipped due to a lack of confidence.

I was riddled with shame and embarrassment, having to tell my fiancé that I needed his help after I took so much pride in making so much money and being successful. Shame told me I should have known better, should have managed my money better, and that my fiancé would be so disappointed in me. I was also afraid he was going to confirm my fears about running my own business and that I didn't know what I was doing - imposter syndrome induced by shame, which kept me from asking him sooner than I did.

All that drama, and he said of course it was fine, no worries, don't be upset. He even mentioned that I had just gone full-time in my business less than a year ago, and this was my first financially hard month in a very, very long time.

All that shame and guilt because I was listening to my inner imposter, and letting shame silence me. I was *so* afraid that someone would be disappointed in me, so I could rationalize being disappointed in myself.

But disappointment, much like all emotions we've discussed over the past couple of chapters, can't hurt us. It might be very uncomfortable, and we might make it mean everything about us...but we are physically going to be okay. You can remind your brain of that - I am okay. This doesn't have to mean anything unless I make it mean something.

Give yourself permission to feel disappointed without attaching your worth. Remember that disappointment will want to lead you to shame for "being bad" - but shame isn't welcome at the party. Disappointment can stay for as long as you need to feel it and let it pass. And then let's get back to business.

The Disappointment Process

1. Allow yourself to have a pity party. Light some candles, journal it out, walk around your house and cry - but set a timer for no more than 30 minutes. You can also air it out with a coach or a therapist. Validate yourself.

2. Ask yourself, "What story am I telling myself about this disappointment?" Most importantly, **what do you think it means about you?**

3. List out 25 *(yes, 25)* reasons why it's a good thing you're feeling your way through this disappointment, what you've learned, what it will do for you - how is the disappointment good?

Remember the rule - *always* validate yourself before you reframe.

Now, go and disappoint someone so you can put this into practice. I vote for you to disappoint your parents, that's an easy one.

Perfectionism Only Sounds Good on a Resume

Breaking up with perfectionism is what helped me write this book.

I wouldn't consider it a clean break. It's more like when you move out of your hometown and away from your ex, but then you come home for the holidays and you text him, you hook up, and then you feel like shit and question everything, until you go back to where you live and come to your senses.

Perfectionism is covering up deeply rooted imposter syndrome. I also think that perfectionism is the mark of an extremely fragile existence.

Perfectionism covers up deeply rooted imposter syndrome because if you're not perfect, it means that you aren't good enough.

And if someone else comes to the realization you're not good enough through witnessing your mistakes or your failures, you are suddenly faced with this realization, too *(which is your biggest fear).*

And then, you will feel something. Shame, disappointment, hurt, sadness. You already know that we avoid these feelings and anything that we suspect will bring on these feelings.

So, perfectionism swoops in to save the day. If we focus on getting it right and getting it tight, we won't have to worry about being found out and therefore we won't have to worry about hurting our own feelings. We also won't have to worry about being rejected.

Perfectionism lives under the guise of protection, when it is really an act of avoidance to experiencing anything. *Like, anything at all.*

To live is to feel. Experience comes from taking action. Perfectionism sounds good on a resume, but it operates under the premise that there is a metric for **good enough,** and you need to achieve it. Except you don't get any rules or an outline. It is just an arbitrary idea in the back of your mind, parading around as attainable.

Good enough is completely and utterly subjective. The problem is, in your job, in your life, in your relationships - you are on a constant quest to be good enough, and you always end up deciding that whatever you are or whatever you did, was in fact, not good enough.

The problem isn't that you're not good enough and you need to figure out *how* to be.

The problem is that you think that "good enough" can be measured.

I stack the dishwasher in an entirely different way than my fiancé does. His way is obviously the wrong way, but I digress.

If someone were to come into my house and stack our dishwasher, it would entirely depend upon who's looking at the dishwasher to decide if it was "good enough" or not. Even if we used the term "perfect" - what's perfect to my fiancé looks like ass-crap to me.

Good enough is in the eye of the beholder. The catch is that when you truly don't feel good enough, nothing you do will ever be enough in your eyes.

Perfectionism is a form of protecting yourself. It's a coping mechanism, a way you keep yourself safe, and provides you with a false sense of control.

If you can be all of the things, do all of the things, and do those things *well* - then you're perfect. And if you're perfect, you're good enough.

Okay Jill.... And? What's wrong with wanting to be perfect? What's wrong with wanting to be the best?

Because what you're actually seeking is love & validation. And when you're afraid you might not get it, you will perfect and prune and edit and wait...until you feel like it's enough. Except it will never be enough.

When I first started my business, I spent my night shifts at my full-time job working on my website. I finished my Master's in September 2017 and was working on my website literally the next week.

But I didn't "launch" my business until January 19, 2018. I was consumed with making my website perfect before I launched, and then I did, and I heard absolute crickets *(which is obviously very normal for someone without an audience yet)*.

When I launched my website, I didn't feel ready. I have never felt ready for anything in my business whatsoever. The only thing that's changed is that I now know that good enough doesn't exist except in my mind, and my mind is clouded by impossibly high expectations and stories from my past that my brain makes literally anything I do insufficient.

It is just a story that my very conditioned neural pathways have adopted. My "I'm not good enough" story, my imposter syndrome story, the ones that *always* live under the mask of perfectionism.

I once had a friend say that she doesn't struggle with perfectionism, because she doesn't think anything she does is perfect.

But most people who struggle with perfectionism *don't* value themselves or think highly of their work. They call themselves perfectionists because they avoid and work on and *perfect* the things that they do because they don't believe it's good enough to begin with.

At the core of it - you don't feel good enough, and therefore your work or what you create never feels good enough, either.

Good Enough is a magical and very fake place. It is a land with unicorns *(my fave)* and fairies. You could try to find it, but you'll never be able to - because it only exists as an arbitrary idea in your mind.

Before you learn to overcome imposter syndrome, you truly believe that Good Enough is a real place. You spend your days trying to find it in jobs, friends, lovers, hobbies, and everywhere else.

If Good Enough *was* a place, it would be in a different location for everyone. Good enough *means* something different to everyone. My Good Enough is very different from your Good Enough.

Once you learn to overcome imposter syndrome, you realize that Good Enough is a magical land that only exists in your mind. And then you realize that Good Enough is a feeling. It is your thoughts and feelings that create the Good Enough place.

When you get specific on what is good enough and what perfection means, it stops becoming such a mystery. When you seek out specifics and details instead of living in vagueness and ambiguity, it stops becoming unknown territory.

For example - what does a perfectly written book look like? What does it have? What does it say?

I had thoughts about not being good enough to write a book, and they kept me paralyzed in inaction for years, despite being an avid reader and writer for my entire life. I won writing awards in school and was always recognized for my written work. Yet, I thought writing a book would be an ultimate feat I could never accomplish.

It is no surprise to me that in doing the inner work, looking at my limiting beliefs and disproving them, learning to fully accept myself, and overcoming imposter syndrome, it led me to start putting my phalanges to the keys on my laptop and write this book for you.

When I learned that my "I'm not good enough" story could be rewritten and I actually *was* capable of anything I put my mind to, even if I had the limitations and the past experiences that told me I wasn't...I didn't internalize my shame about feeling unworthy. I started to problem solve.

What exactly was the perfect book? What did I think was worthy of being published? What did I think was good enough?

As I became more and more specific in my internal questioning whenever a limiting thought popped up that was just another flavour of "You can't write a book", I began to realize that I could do whatever the fuck I want.

I could write a book in whatever order I wanted, with whatever stories I wanted. I could make it funny, put "fuck" in wherever I wanted, and I could also include research and evidence to support my claims if that's what I wanted to do.

Perfection doesn't exist, just like the land of Good Enough doesn't exist. If Good Enough is a feeling, Perfection is a thought.

You can decide to think, "This is perfect as it is."

You can decide to think "It's not perfect, but what is perfect anyway? I can fix it up if I need to."

In 2016, a couple of friends and I went to Chicago for the weekend. We went to the Art Institute of Chicago, and yes, art is beautiful. But I was more enamored by the fact that I was surrounded by so many paintings done by people who just *decided* their work was good enough to share with the world. What is perfect or good enough, even, when you look at art? You'll never find the answer, because beauty (and good enough) is in the eye of the beholder.

Listen, impossibly high standards are normal for a person who feels like a fraud, and perfectionism is just whispering in your ear, telling you that those impossible standards are very much possible, and you're just not achieving them because of who you are.

But remember, your thoughts are a dialogue - not a Ted Talk. You are learning to observe your thoughts and question them, instead of just deciding that they're true. When perfectionism comes up, aim to get specific. What do I think will be good enough? What am I measuring perfection with? Are my standards about doing a good job, or are they actually about looking a certain way and proving my worth?

I once did one of those Paint & Wine Nights with a girlfriend, and let me tell you, the instructor had to fix my palm trees. I am not a painter by any means, but I choose to see myself and carry myself as an artist through my writing despite my inability to use a paint brush. Artists are creative, and they do not aim to be bound by rules or standards or by how things "should" be.

I have a tattoo that is a quote from One Tree Hill, my favourite show when I was a teenager. One of the main characters, Peyton Sawyer, says "Your art matters". It always resonated with me, because getting your art into the world has to come from the belief that it matters and deserves to be put into the world. And that always starts with you believing you're good enough.

It doesn't matter what your job is or if you own a business - choose to be the creator of your life. Choose to recognize that perfection and good enough will always be unattainable if you let someone else define them for you.

Take the power back by learning how to define these things for yourself.

Take the power back by questioning your thoughts and taking the time to inquire about what your brain means when it asks for things to be perfect and good enough.

This will get easier with time, and it will get easier as you overcome imposter syndrome and continue on your worthiness journey.

Rejection: It's Going to Feel Like You're Dying Even Though You're Not

All my life, I never felt like I was "chosen".

I chalk this up to a couple of things. I'm the middle child. I was never picked first for sports *(which was fair, I wasn't very good)*. I never felt like I was someone's **best** friend; it felt like someone always came before me.

And when I was chosen, I didn't like *why* I was chosen. Like when my grade four teacher gave me special treatment and everyone called me teacher's pet. Or when my speech therapist would come to the door of my classroom and everyone would look at me as I begrudgingly went with her so I could do speech exercises that involved me talking really fucking slow.... like at a speed that no one would talk at, ever.

The point of the matter is I wanted to be chosen, but not in the spotlight. I wanted to be important, but not seen. I had written a story for a school book fair, and I had included the word "crestfallen" to describe how a character looked. I was in the sixth grade. A boy who was a year older than me came up and asked if I knew what it meant, and I was so embarrassed I just walked away. I wanted to be noticed, but when I actually was noticed, it felt like a too-hot spotlight on all of the reasons why I didn't like myself.

It doesn't really matter how anybody else interpreted these experiences that I had. My friends will tell you it's not true I wasn't chosen and my mom will definitely be butt hurt that I joke about being the forgotten middle child. But at the end of the day, no matter what happened, that was how I experienced these things because of my very low self-worth, and my decreasing sense of worthiness as I became older and older.

When you don't feel good enough, you will feel this way, too. You want to be chosen, but at the same time, being seen can be scary - because both things put you at the risk of rejection.

I often see this with my clients in my coaching practice. When they're trying to sign clients into their own businesses, they feel not good enough or unworthy if someone doesn't want to work with them - they feel rejected. In the same breath, as they grow their business and become bigger and make more money, they sometimes freeze up because it means that more people will see their stuff and be exposed to them - which puts my client at the risk of feeling rejected.

Rejection feels like a certain death to our caveman brains. It *is* the equivalent to death, as when you were outed, excluded, or separated from the pack hundreds of years ago, you were more than likely going to die.

That was in reference to a depletion of food and resources.

But now, our risks are in reference to validation, love, and belonging. And the risk of losing those things and losing that sense of "safety" is scary, because we still haven't evolved from the brain's basic needs.

Our brains can't comprehend the complexity of someone on social media not liking our opinion and calling us out - so it rings the alarm like it would if we were in *actual* danger.

But Jill, how will building your self-worth and realizing that you're good enough help with rejection, when rejection is quite literally a reality at all times?

Rejection is only painful because of what we make it mean about ourselves when it happens. Meaning, that when we are rejected, we make it mean something that is related to *why* we feel unworthy.

And now, I introduce to you - Your Perceived Colossal Flaw (AKA your PCF).

In her book, The Secret Thoughts of Successful Women, Dr. Valerie Young[10] talks about imposter syndrome and what she calls your "crusher" - the thing that if someone found out about you, it would absolutely crush you.

My take on this is the **Perceived Colossal Flaw**; something that you believe is flawed about you, and something that you believe if someone were to find out about you, they would know "too much" and make a negative determination about you.

But the thing is, it's perceived only by *you* as a colossal flaw; hence, why it's your *perceived* colossal flaw and not just your colossal flaw.

The stories we tell ourselves about our character, our actions,

[10] *The Secret Thoughts of Successful Women, Dr. Valerie Young, 2011*

our traits, our mental illness, our disabilities, our hindrances - they are just stories that we continually perpetuate. Remember that because our brains are prone to confirmation bias, our subconscious mind is actively seeking out all information that will support what we believe. This also means it may be missing or discarding information that proves our stories otherwise.

For me, my PCF was my stuttering disability. The story of "Because I stutter, I'm not good enough" was created very early in my childhood. Children (and adults) that didn't know any better would laugh at me. I would become hyper-attuned to the discomfort of others when I was stuttering, so I either sped up what I was saying or just didn't speak altogether to avoid seeing their discomfort. I would stutter in class during speeches that they made us do from grade 4 on, and I could feel the hot heat of embarrassment, desperately wanting to escape. As I got older, I developed coping mechanisms by avoiding introducing myself to people and hoping someone else would introduce me, and leaving the room pretending to be coughing or having to pee if we had to go around the room in classrooms or job onboarding sessions. I'd go through the drive-thru only if I was alone, I wouldn't share my ideas in meetings, and I even started my coaching business out of the idea that I would have total control over where and when I spoke *(I came to realize that I am literally public speaking all the time for my business - on my podcast, on my social media, guest speaking engagements, coaching calls, networking events - so the joke was on me)*

I repeatedly told myself the story of, "Because I stutter, I'm not good enough", and that is what I deduced from every single encounter and experience I had where my stutter took center stage. And it did take center stage, because it was all I could think about, all of the time.

It was my PCF, not because I thought I could hide it from anyone *(eventually, they would find out)* but because I was afraid of what they would think about me once they knew that I stuttered or once they experienced me stuttering in front of them.

Because here's what I thought about my stutter - it was ugly. It made me sound stupid. I didn't like being labeled as someone with a disability. I'm not normal because I stutter. I'm not attractive because I stutter. People will find me annoying.

My now fiancé and I started dating in the ninth grade, and a mutual friend of ours said to him, "You know she stutters, right?" That *crushed* me, and just furthered the story that because of my stutter, I wasn't good enough. Also, my fiancé looked like Zac Efron, and High School Musical is my love language. So the "I'm not attractive because I stutter" really came out there.

Your PCF can quite literally be anything, and it could be multiple things - but the point is, if you were to boil down most of your experiences and why you think you can't be something, accomplish something, or why you're afraid for someone to really see you and know you - it's somehow related to your PCF, and it's at the core of why you don't believe you're good enough.

Understanding *what* exactly you're afraid of people finding out about you will help you desensitize yourself to this fear of rejection. You may have some insights on this from the shadow work portion we did in the chapter about shame.

You know how people say that when you name something, you take its power away? That's how you should feel about your

PCF. And that's how you should approach rejection - because it's going to feel like dying, but that's just your prehistoric brain being a prehistoric dummy. You are not going to die if you're rejected - I promise.

There will be instances of rejection, sure. But the brain, in addition to being prehistoric, is also a drama queen. It will take an experience that *feels* like a rejection and sound the alarms like you're dying.

For example - you might be an entrepreneur using social media to promote your business, and you might post a polarizing opinion - and then someone comments that they disagree with you. You may start to feel anxious and panicked - and that's because your brain has already rushed to the worst case scenario, and it believes you've been separated from the pack and now you're going to die. You're going to be outed as a fraud because someone disagrees with you and now everything is going to go to shit.

But it's just an Instagram comment from *one* person. You might get sweaty, uncomfortable, you might start shaming yourself, you might spin out - but you're not going to die.

When you feel like a fraud, when you don't feel good enough - rejection does in fact feel fatal. If the collective agrees that you're not perfect or that you did something wrong, you're more at risk of being "found out".

But remember - you are infinitely worthy and good enough. Your fear of being found out isn't grounded in reality - it's grounded in your perceived experience of not being good enough, when that's not the ultimate truth.

Just like your *perceived* colossal flaw - it is only a colossal flaw to *you*.

What if rejection didn't kill you?

What if you *felt* rejection all the way through to the other side, as if it was an emotion in your body?

Because truly, that's what it's demanding of us. If the fear of rejection is so potent inside of us all because of the way our brains function, why wouldn't we treat it like an emotion and allow ourselves to feel it so we can learn, time and time again, that it isn't fatal to feel it?

Here's a five-step process I created in 2019 called **The Rejection Template**. Take the last time you felt rejected, passed over, dismissed - and do this exercise now by journaling out your response to these questions:

1. Take the situation you experienced. How can you look at this situation as neutrally as possible? What are just the facts of the situation, not what you thought or felt about it?

2. What did you make this mean about yourself? Are these things ultimately true?

3. What past experiences did this situation trigger for you? Is it possible you're reacting from a past experience that you don't need to put on this current situation?

4. What are the possible alternatives to what *you* think this rejection meant? Write down at least 5 different ways this "rejection" could be interpreted. *For example: A person said no to your program, but it's more so about them and their financial situation than about you and what you did wrong.*

5. What are the lessons you can learn from this rejection that will improve your life/business/career, etc? Write down at least 10 lessons learned.

You Could Never Be Found Out

There is nothing anyone could ever find out about you that would render you unworthy or not good enough.

By this point, you realize that the actual experience of being "found out" isn't real, it is more so how you think you will feel. But emotions can't hurt you, and you could never be "found out". You don't need to walk on eggshells, hold yourself back, play small, or keep your knowledge and expertise hidden from the world.

It's admirable, really, that you're so consumed with being "found out". It means you care about the work you're doing. It means you think others deserve the best of you. It means you're not scamming anyone. It means you put deliberate thought and effort into who you want to be. It means you picked up this book because you believe feeling worthy and good enough won't only serve you, but everyone around you, too.

Your willingness to find your worthiness is an indicator that it's there.

Keep going.

Failure is an Illusion

There is no failure.

Ever.

You only fail if you give up.

Yeah, you can fuck things up.

You can hear no a million times.

You can miss the mark or the deadline.

You can be back at the beginning of a very tiring journey that you were almost finished with.

But failure is only perceived as the end when you *decide* it's the end.

After making multiple six figures in my business, I found myself driving around for Uber Eats for extra cash because I hadn't made any new sales in a couple of months, and I still had some credit card debt I was working on getting down.

I felt like I failed. I even cried to my fiancé several times, asking him if he thought I was a failure, one eye squinting at him, waiting for the certain impact of him agreeing that I was a failure and needed to pack it in. Go home, Jill, your inner imposter was RIGHT.

He obviously comforted me and repeatedly told me he was proud of me and my resourcefulness, and that no, I wasn't a failure. But I felt like one.

My feelings were valid, and it was understandable why I felt that way.

But you know the drill. Just because I felt that way didn't mean it was the truth.

I was not a failure. Failure is impossible when you are certain of an outcome and keep working towards it, no matter what gets in your way or tries to stop you.

Life is short, but it's also very long. You will have many different experiences and endeavors in your life. The ending of something does not signify a failure.

Every experience is neutral. But you get to decide what to think about it.

I chose to see my little stint with Uber Eats as a part of my entrepreneurial journey. I chose to see it as a testament to my faith in myself and my willingness to be resourceful. I chose to zoom out and see those two months as the tiniest blip in my journey.

When I went to university for my Bachelor's, my fiancé and I did long distance for four years. At the time, those four years felt like a lifetime, and in the moment, I would think of how hard it was. But when I zoomed out and looked at the entirety of our relationship, I knew that four years would feel like nothing.

This is how you can reframe failure

1. Think of the perceived "failure" as just a hurdle you had to overcome.
2. Don't make the hurdle mean anything about your worth or where you're going.
3. Continue to live your life.

Self-Acceptance is The Bare Fucking Minimum

In a session with a new coaching client, she expressed frustration that she had been "working" on herself for years and hadn't seen "results".

I asked what her outcome was. What was the point of doing all this work on herself?

She didn't have an answer.

The answer is this: you do everything you do, to love yourself more.

But when that sounds and feels like utter bullshit, self-acceptance is and should be the bare fucking minimum.

Think about the weight that was lifted from your shoulders when you heard that so many other people don't feel good enough, too. Or that 70% of people struggle with imposter syndrome. Or when a friend says, "Omg, I've been ghosted too."

My business coach would coach me on money, and I always felt so much shame about it - until she told us that in the community she was in, where people were making millions of dollars, the #1 thing everyone would talk about is their fears and insecurities around money.

Earlier in this book, you learned that validating your experiences is the key to moving forward from what holds you back.

And the reason why you validate yourself is so you can accept yourself.

This is what happens when you accept yourself:

- You don't feel ashamed of what you like or enjoy doing.
- You feel more comfortable sharing your opinions.
- You live in the present moment more.
- You enjoy and are grateful for little things.
- You allow yourself to rest and relax.
- You become more optimistic.
- You believe you can achieve what you set your mind to.

This can all happen as a result of self-acceptance. Meaning, you don't even have to fully love yourself in order to live a happy, soul-liberating, good enough-feeling life.

When you accept yourself, you silently project that to others.

And others will say, "She's confident."

A viewer once said to Oprah[11], "Watching you be yourself

---

[11] *Oprah Reflects by Daily Post Staff, 2011*

makes me want to be more myself."

Confidence is just self-acceptance that others can see. Because you've made the internal decision that you're good enough.

When I didn't have any confidence in myself, I was actively trying to get rid of my stutter. I begged my mom to buy a VHS set when I was 13 that declared that I could "Stop Stuttering NOW". I applied to my university's disability program 4 times before they granted me $10,000 to buy the SpeechEasy, a tiny device that went in my ear and projected a voice to speak in unison with me. I bought coaching programs, went to a hypnotist, and listened to subliminal frequencies on YouTube.

This was all because I believed that my stutter was something I couldn't accept about myself. Hence, I thought that the only way to feel confident was to get rid of it.

I thought it was one or the other - I either got rid of my stutter or I learned to love it. When I learned to meet in the middle at self-acceptance is when my confidence grew.

I didn't have to love my stutter, but I could accept it. This doesn't mean it was *easy* to accept it, but all I needed to believe was that it was possible for me to accept who I was without actually needing to "get rid" of my stutter or without needing to love it.

The reason why you might struggle with accepting yourself is because your previous acceptance of self has relied purely on external validation. Remember, unworthiness is a rite of passage, and finding your worthiness is a journey. And on that journey, as a kid and then as a teenager, your sense of identity may have been formulated by other people.

As a little girl, I often heard from well-meaning adults that "it's a good thing you're pretty, Jilli". This was if I didn't understand something, or made a dumb comment, or couldn't figure something out right away.

Again, these people were well-meaning and saying it in jest, but I learned that my only value was in my looks *(and I wasn't even confident in those, either).* I learned that I wasn't smart. I learned that I had to immediately understand things or know how to do something or it meant something about my intelligence level.

We don't actively look around and say, "Tell me who I am". But what other choice do we have than to see ourselves through the eyes of others? If we are not taught to trust our judgment or to value our own opinions, it makes sense why we'd look to others to tell us who we are.

Another block to your self-acceptance may be that you've always felt wrong. This is an imposter-y thing that I really found in my entrepreneur clients who had a hard time being creative and coming up with their own intellectual property. They didn't feel good enough, and as a result, will never think that what they create is good enough.

What you create comes from your brain. So if you don't feel fundamentally worthy, your work won't feel worthy, either. And if you have consistently felt like you've had to prove yourself and your opinion, if you often felt questioned or misunderstood in your earlier years - you may have developed the belief that others know better than you. And this can be seriously activated when you work for yourself or enter into a high-level position, because once you are responsible for making rules, making decisions, and being a thought leader - you might really struggle with imposter syndrome because you've been conditioned to believe the answers are outside of you.

I had the hardest time creating concepts, strategies, and processes for my clients in the beginning of my business because I didn't think that I knew what worked. I had the constant question in my mind if I was giving them the "right" information, and I often looked to other "experts" in my space to inform my thinking.

Overcoming imposter syndrome and stepping into my worthiness looked like owning my opinions, and deciding that what I knew and the experience I had was good enough. And that *had* to come from being fully and completely accepting of myself and who I was.

Another reason why self-acceptance is just confidence that others can see is because there is minimal impact if someone disagrees with you, calls you out for your opinion, or straight up thinks you're wrong.

You don't overreact, and you don't spin out. You're confident in who you are and what you know, but you can also accept that you don't have to be perfect and that others have different experiences than you and therefore, may draw different conclusions.

Let's take writing a book as an example. There are *so* many tools, tips, tricks, and strategies when it comes to the writing process. But while there are a lot of ways to write a book, there is no *right* way.

Your process is your own. And chances are, your process will resonate with a lot of people. But someone else's way will resonate with a lot of other people, and maybe that process is completely opposite to yours.

The bottom line is, it doesn't matter what way is right and

what way is wrong. Humans are completely subjective at all times. We're biased, and like I've been saying this whole time, hypocritical.

You are allowed to decide that you are good enough and what you decide to create is good enough. There is no person who is following behind you, making sure that you are doing things "the right way".

A lot of prominent people in history would have never made history if they did things how they were always done. And what do all of these people have in common? They accepted themselves and their art or what they did as *good enough*.

Like when I visited The Art Institute of Chicago - think about an art gallery, and all the weird, wonderful, abstract, funky things that you'd find there. They all have something in common - their artist believed their work was good enough, and put it out into the world.

So, we started with understanding where your thoughts and beliefs originated from, and we validated your experiences. We covered things that you will inevitably hit up against at all times in your journey, like shame, perfectionism, failure, and rejection.

This next step is self-acceptance. Can you accept yourself for who you are, right now, in this moment?

Because hear me when I say - nobody is going to save you. You have to be the hero of your own story. As much as relationships and connections are pivotal to our mental and emotional health...

No one will ever give a fuck about you as much as *you* should give a fuck about you.

This isn't isolating. It's liberating. It's liberating to choose yourself. It's liberating to decide to take matters into your own hands. It's liberating to take action and be responsible for everything that happens in your life.

"I'm not good enough" is just another flavor of "I don't feel chosen". When we don't feel chosen, we wonder why we haven't been chosen.

This showed up for me in my online coaching business. If a client didn't hire me after being interested in my services, I'd take it personally that they didn't "choose" me (and felt even worse when I knew they had chosen a different coach over me).

But I was unconsciously deciding each day to not choose myself. To believe that I didn't have the right answers, that someone knew better than me, that something about me was the reason I didn't have what I wanted.

You might walk around and demand that others show their love for you so you can decide that you're acceptable enough to be loved. You might outright demand affection and attention, or you might read signals and clues and misinterpret them as reasons why people don't care about you *(I've done both)*.

None of it will matter. Because if you don't give a fuck about yourself - their fucks won't land. They might for a moment, but then they'll be dissolving fucks. You will eventually go on to try and find more and more fucks from others, but they won't be enough. Because all the fucks in the world will never be as solid, safe, stable, and consistent as The Fuck you give about yourself.

You want to make the journey back to worthiness and the process of loving yourself less cringey? Start by looking in the mirror and pointing at yourself, saying "I give a fuck about you." Add "bitch" if you're feeling spicy. You'll probably laugh. It might make you cry.

Giving a fuck about yourself is safe. It doesn't require the validation or acceptance of anyone else. You just get to decide you are worthy of the bare minimum - support, care, and self-acceptance.

Self-acceptance *is* the bare minimum in your worthiness journey. No shame in your game if that's where you're starting, because there's nowhere to go but up.

How to Accept Yourself

What things would you change about yourself?

What do you cringe about?

What do you think you could do better?

And now, imagine that you have a best friend or a little sister or someone you love the fuck out of. You've known this person your entire life. You'd do anything for them and believe that they're a good, pure-hearted person who has your back. And you have theirs. You know they're not perfect, but you can't imagine them holding back their light, holding back their ideas, or thinking that they're not good enough.

Now, imagine that the person is **you**.

Safety & Worthiness are Feelings You Have, Not Things You Achieve

My fiancé, Dustin, and I have been together for fifteen years at the time of my writing this book in 2022. I turned 30 years old this year, so yes, that means we've been together for half of our lives.

Dustin has seen me go from a young, awkward teenager with very little self-worth, to a capable, confident, and successful woman with a multiple 6-figure business. (I'm still very awkward, though). And something that I love about him is that he has always been my steady home base.

I'm well aware that not everyone has a person they'd consider a home base; but what I'm talking about is more so the feeling of **safety**. Feeling safe has allowed me to fly. Safety, I've discovered, really is a *feeling*.

Our brains and our bodies, especially those of us with anxiety and other mental health issues, struggle to feel safe even when there are no physical threats to harm us. But just like when I look to my fiancé to be one of my home bases when everything else gets crazy as fuck - I think we should turn to our internal sense of safety, which I believe is synonymous with worthiness.

When I don't feel good enough, there is a sense of panic. Of fear. Of anxiety.

When I feel worthy, I feel at home. Peaceful. Safe. Confident in myself.

I think confidence feels safe, too. It feels safe because you are more apt to take risks and put yourself out of your comfort zone when you know that there is a safety net behind you. Many would say that the safety net is bad - but I think it just depends on what your safety net is, and if it's there out of fear or not.

But the caveat here is that learning how to feel worthy is like learning how to do your taxes. You're doing it, all the while thinking "Is this it? Am I doing it right? What's this new thing I have to do? Fuck, I thought I had a handle on this. Well, this feels shitty. Again, am I doing it right?! Is anyone going to tell me how to do this?"

Like so many people who live paycheck to paycheck, I dreamed about the day that my business was making enough money where I could pay all my bills and my debt and have money left over. What I was really craving was the feeling of being safe - and even though the money came, and I was making more money than ever before, I didn't feel safe. I still felt scarce, anxious, and my problems went from trying to make money to trying to make more of it.

For many people with imposter syndrome, a lack of safety is what feels most normal to them. This can also be seen as the

Productivity Wound - when you're addicted to achieving, but rarely give yourself time or space to celebrate what you've achieved. This goes along with thoughts of never feeling good enough, no matter what you achieve, because remember - imposter syndrome is a dysfunctional way of thinking, not a revelation of the truth. Because you are so used to thinking like an imposter, it makes sense that an external event, like achieving a goal, will only give you temporary reprieve until you're onto the next thing to prove your worth.

People with imposter syndrome believe that their worth is always in the future because they're discontented with the present. **Underneath it all, it is the need to be somewhere that is not "here", because you don't believe that you are "safe" here.**

It's like a reverse nostalgia, really. The brain is a fickle thing; you will crave the past because you believed you felt good and happy and safe "back then", but in reality, you were probably dealing with some bull shit, probably telling yourself you could make more money, probably wishing for the next day or project or thing to come.

This is another way your brain keeps you unsatisfied with the present moment - by leading you to believe there was or is a different moment where you feel All The Things You Want to Feel. But that moment never lives in the past, even though your brain romanticizes it. And it never lives in the future, unless you plan on creating it. All We Have Is Now, and that means safety is something we must learn how to feel right now, even amidst everything that feels unsafe, all of the time.

There's a reason why self-actualization is at the top of Maslow's Hierarchy of Needs - it is rendered unnecessary to find one's true purpose or discover who we are unless a person has their basic needs met. Safety is a basic need - but now that we are safe from physical danger 99.9% of the time, unlike times when physical danger was an everyday concern and humans had to be hypervigilant so they didn't die - internal safety is a basic need, and that includes protecting our self-concept and what we think about ourselves so we can save ourselves from any kind of emotional discomfort.

It makes sense that in order for us to branch out and put ourselves in situations that would uplevel our lives even though they may be a little scary, that we would have to do those things from a place of internal safety.

Internal safety is trust in yourself. It is the inner knowing that no matter what happens, you will have your own back.

If you would have asked me in 2020 to leave my job to take my business full-time, I would have thrown up on the spot. I have a visceral memory of being at a meeting at my job that year, before the pandemic hit and we all started working from home. My brain went to the thought of, "One day you'll be working for yourself" and I felt sick to my stomach. I couldn't imagine leaving to be my own boss, and I used to say I had to wait to pay off all my debt, buy a house, and have a fuck ton of savings before I could do it.

I left in May 2021. I had no savings and still had debt and the real estate market is absolutely bonkers where I live, so no house either. It didn't matter. I felt a literal pull from the universe. I bawled my eyes out for days. I consulted every single one of my friends, who I knew would push me to do it, and didn't tell my parents until after I did it, because I knew they'd have hesitations. But my inner knowing was strong. I was going to be okay. **And even if I wasn't okay, I would be.**

Knowing what's right for you and having your own back can be really difficult as a person with imposter syndrome, especially if you've primarily lived in the realm of "everyone knows better than me".

You may have been able to rationalize this as a child. You genuinely didn't know better when you were young and expendable and malleable. But now, you are a whole-ass adult that pays taxes and is in charge of things like keeping pets, children, and plants alive, and remembering to schedule your annual pap smear.

It is time for you to start a) trusting yourself, and b) deciding that you know what's best for you. From there, internal safety is more than possible - it's an everyday reality.

Your subconscious doesn't want this off the hop, of course. Because believing you don't know best offsets responsibility, accountability, and ownership. It presents as imposter syndrome and not feeling good enough - but it actually feels *good* to be the victim, it feels *good* to not be held accountable for things that happen to you. *This* is the sense of safety that we want to avoid, because it is largely due to dissatisfaction and "there's nothing I can do about it" kind of energy. Like "I know the answer but I'm not going to raise my hand" kind of energy.

The desire to be unaccountable is present because we never want to be responsible for our own pain and suffering, and we'd rather fork ourselves in the eye than be responsible for the pain and suffering of someone else. I used to give advice to my friends and then say, "I don't know, though" just so I wasn't responsible for when my own advice went to shit.

But my friends are smart, capable, and worthy humans. And they are just as responsible for their own lives and happiness as I am for mine.

There are no wrong paths or wrong answers. There are only decisions, and then where that decision takes you. Like a Choose Your Own Adventure book - what if you believed that no matter what, you'd get to the end of the story exactly how you were supposed to? That whatever decision you made, it would be okay. If you are willing to feel anything that comes your way, if you are willing to have your own back and not shame yourself for the decisions you've made or will make - how could you *not* feel safe?

Safety comes from a feeling inside of your body that reverberates "I am okay." Right now, as you are. Even without all the money you'd like in your bank account. Even without knowing what your next step is. Even without apologizing to your sister for snapping at her when you were overstimulated. **If you are always chasing external things in order to feel "okay", you will truly never be okay.**

Safe and worthy are feelings you have because in order to receive more, you have to be okay (read: grateful) with what you currently have. So much about our society is centered around and teaches us about hustling, goal-setting, and achievement as markers for worth. But for what purpose do we achieve? For what purpose do we do the things to achieve the things?

To feel happy. For fulfillment. And at the end of the day, to go to sleep feeling safe and content and okay.

And from that place of feeling safe, you can take risks, step outside of your comfort zone, say the crazy shit, do the cringey thing - and get everything you've ever wanted.

How to Feel Safe:

- Go to www.jillianparekh.com/yns-book and find the "Creating Safety in the Body" meditation.
- Find a comfortable place to sit, close your eyes, and complete the meditation.
- Do this each and everyday so you can identify what safe feels like to you and your body, and how to return to that place of stability.

Safe & Comfortable Are Two Different Things

Yes, feeling safe and secure in our bodies is extremely important, and that's why we spent so much time talking about it.

But now, you're coming into your own. You're getting ready to make moves, take action, and go after what you want because you realized you can feel worthy of having whatever you want.

But you're going to be uncomfortable a lot of the time. Do not mistake discomfort with being unsafe.

The reason why you may not be able to tell the difference is because your anxiety and fears have never been investigated or pulled up from their roots until now. I was diagnosed with Generalized Anxiety Disorder in addition to ADHD, and the stomachaches I used to get everyday before school, the way I would literally leave a room if I thought we had to introduce ourselves at school, the way I would pretend to have homework to do at lunch so I didn't have to be in the cafeteria alone if my friends weren't there - it all made sense. I have anxiety, and this created a perpetual feeling of being unsafe.

You may not be diagnosed with anxiety, but anxious thoughts are very common for the majority of people. And when we don't know why we're experiencing anxiety or fear, we assign "safe" and "unsafe" to certain situations, and then avoid them or dread them at all costs.

But when you're starting a business, or a new job, or going to a wedding, or doing *anything* where you're living your life and putting yourself out there, it is so important for your brain to be able to decipher between "I am uncomfortable" and "I am unsafe".

It's very simple - when you are in a situation where you start to feel unsteady and unsure about yourself, when the anxious thoughts come rushing in, ask yourself, "Am I unsafe or just a little uncomfortable?"

More often than not, you will be uncomfortable, unless you are in physical danger. And when you notice you are uncomfortable, take stock of why: maybe you're about to do a presentation at work. Maybe you're about to start with a new client. Maybe you're putting boundaries in place for the first time. **Discomfort doesn't mean anything has gone wrong and it doesn't mean you need to fix or change anything.**

From a foundational place of worthiness, from a place of a sturdy self-concept, the question of "Am I unsafe or just a little uncomfortable?" will change your life. Because the truth is, whenever we're going after our dreams, doing something new, putting ourselves out there - it will be uncomfortable at first. Do it anyway. You are safe. You are good enough.

The Debilitating Fear of Being Seen

As a 30-year-old woman who has stuttered her entire life, I am acutely aware as to how much space I am taking up.

At an early age, I learned that I should speak really fast or not speak at all. I could feel the air in the room when I stuttered and someone was waiting for me to finish. I urge friends and family to do things for me, like tell the restaurant the name of our reservation or recite the drive-thru order, because I don't want to waste anyone's time.

As a kid, I was also super fucking talkative. Looking back this was most likely a sign of my ADHD, but also, I was just a little girl who had a lot to say. I realize now that I was just verbalizing everything I was taking in, instead of internalizing it like I do now.

I primarily market my business through social media, and when I started doing this, I had no idea how much it meant that I had to be comfortable with taking up space. I used to marvel at space takers, while also judging the fuck out of them. It seemed like these people were unaware and not embarrassed at all about the space they were occupying. I wondered, "*How is this person not afraid that someone is going to say to them 'No one gives a fuck!!!'*" I couldn't believe that someone would *dare* share their opinions and thoughts as if they were soooo important.

When I didn't have a business, making myself as small as possible also looked like people-pleasing. I dubbed myself and my problems as insignificant. Everything and everyone else was more important than me, and I quickly deflected whenever the focus *was* on me. When I talked to friends, I always put the focus and conversation on them, and felt uncomfortable when they asked about me. If I had an issue, I was so steeped in shame that I didn't talk about it with anyone whatsoever. My own best friends didn't even know I had so much shame and anxiety about my stutter until a trip to Chicago in 2018 - and they had been my best friends for over a decade at this point.

I was a master at being Insignificant & Unimportant. And then, I started a business where I *had* to be seen. And not just with my face - with my words, with my opinions, with my knowledge and expertise. Being seen was the *only* way I was going to have a thriving business - and I didn't even want to see myself.

Just like the conflicting dialogue in our minds, I believe our inner knowing will lead us to what we truly want to do. Then, we hit a series of tests and roadblocks; the universe's way of saying "Are you sure you want it? Because if you do, you'll have to confront every single thing you dislike about yourself." It's a cruel joke that our most meaningful paths are littered with accepting, and yes, even *loving*, the parts of us that we wish would just stay in the dark.

The concept of being fully seen is very similar to the talks we've had about rejection and failure; you will avoid it because you believe there is something that being seen will reveal, and then you will be devastated. Mortified. Ashamed. Embarrassed. Dead on emotional impact. RIP, bitch.

When I was in grade four, I won the spelling bee at our school. I was about to go onto the citywide competition, but I was too young, so they sent a girl older than me. She messed up on the word pyjamas. I walked around, all high and mighty, telling the story to myself that she was a dumbass *(we watched a lot of That 70's Show and Red Foreman's voice is always in my head when I call someone a dumbass)*, and if I would have been able to go, I would have won that one, too.

But I didn't actually know that pyjamas were spelled with a Y in Canada. I would have spelled it wrong. Because I didn't even *want* to go to the citywide spelling bee. I was so afraid that I'd be seen as an idiot. I liked being in my comfort zone, and I liked feeling like I was fooling everyone.

Being seen in adulthood meant that a lot of my relationships lacked emotional intimacy on my end. I listened to my friends for hours and hours, but didn't divulge as much as I could about my own life, my own fears, or what I was feeling. When I did reveal something, like how much anxiety I had about my stutter, it felt big and scary. I felt way too vulnerable. I was very emotionally vulnerable with my fiancé, because he was the only person who I felt like wouldn't abandon me if I was super honest with him; but even then, I hid parts of myself out of fear and shame.

When we allow ourselves to be seen, questions that loom in our minds are - Will you still love me? Am I okay?

This is why it's so important to create an internal sense of safety, and to work on fully accepting yourself. Yes, connections and relationships are extremely integral to our emotional well-being; but, if you truly do not feel safe with yourself, if you do not truly accept yourself, somebody else's reassurance will fall deaf on your ears.

Allowing yourself to be fully seen is like a horror movie to the woman who feels like an imposter. It feels jarring and unnecessarily uncomfortable. It requires you to take up space, and for you to be okay with occupying that space.

Why boundaries are so difficult for you, a person who feels like a fraud:

In the simplest of terms, boundaries are limits. Emotional boundaries mean knowing what we will or will not accept. When you feel like a fraud and you have a fear of being seen, it is because you feel shame or guilt around who you are, what you deem important, and what you want. Saying "no" or declaring what you want when someone is requesting (or in some cases, demanding) otherwise can be especially difficult for the person who feels like a fraud, because they might risk being seen as someone they feel ashamed to be seen as.

As a baby coach with little experience and a lot of imposter syndrome, my business boundaries were nonexistent. I would respond to clients who messaged me on weekends, I would allow clients to ask more questions even after the timer was up on our calls, and I would allow clients to stay in containers even if they didn't pay me on time. And because I was sensitive to criticism, fragile in my emotional state, and believed I was a fraud, my resentment seemingly came from them "crossing my boundaries"; when in fact, I was not upholding them out of fear of them thinking something about me that I didn't want them to think.

Boundaries are your responsibility to uphold, rather than the responsibility of others to respect them.

My lack of boundaries as a new coach was a rite of passage, just like my unworthiness is. I had to learn why I had trouble holding my boundaries and work through whatever came up so I could begin to uphold them in a way that felt right. My inner imposter made me believe that if I wasn't over-giving, over-generous, and quick to respond, my clients would think I wouldn't care about them. And what is a coach without genuine care for their clients? It stemmed from my belief of being a bad person, because bad people don't care about others. Therefore, I would sacrifice my own mental and emotional wellbeing simply because I was getting paid and wanted to be "seen" as a good person.

I could find flavors of this in my personal relationships as well, like at work when a coworker would dump all over me and use me as an outlet for her relationship, and even though we weren't particularly close, I thought it was my responsibility to listen to her and console her; because it seemed as if nobody else did. Of course, I cared for her, but not to the point of being her unofficial therapist. When I wanted to talk about something in my life one day, she said she had to finish some work and cut me off halfway through our conversation. I was pissed off and resentful, but I realized later it was because I was pissed off with *myself* for not upholding boundaries that protected my emotional and mental health.

When I began to accept myself, I stopped fearing that my clients would see me as a bad person - because I wasn't. I was merely maintaining my emotional & mental health, something that was actually *good* for me to model for them. When I began to accept myself, I calibrated on how I was feeling emotionally and if I had the space to support someone, and leaned into the conversation if I did. If I didn't have the space to support someone, I didn't - and I was okay with it, too.

This wasn't - and isn't - always so easy. Upholding boundaries may be hard if you have assumed the role of the emotional caretaker for whoever in your life needed it. If you've ever felt like you were responsible for someone's emotional wellbeing, and that your emotions were a burden or there wasn't space for you to have them, especially in childhood, it makes sense that you would be afraid to make someone feel bad. If you find yourself the emotional support friend, perhaps you know what it feels like to be abandoned with your thoughts and emotions, so you want to make sure they feel safe and supported by you. If you fear being seen as a bad or uncaring person, your beliefs about what that looks like will override your own emotional & mental needs.

Think back to the beginning of this book; people see everything through a unique lens. Their experiences shape them, their childhood shapes them, their education, their relationships - no person is the same. You cannot assume how someone is going to think or feel based on an action you haven't taken yet. Maybe a friend has vented so much about her ex, that you not responding to her text right away gave her the space to reflect on it by herself and she came to some massive revelation. Maybe your client said they desperately needed you to respond on a Saturday because they were having a crisis, but then resolved the problem themselves and felt triumphant for doing so.

The bottom line here is that we cannot control how other people see us, but we can control how we see ourselves. When we love ourselves, respect ourselves, and accept ourselves, we can take actions and set boundaries that may feel uncomfortable and jarring to our nervous systems because we are humans with good hearts; but then, we can feel comforted by the fact that we have our own back, no matter what happens.

You Are Not Bad

A Money Coach in the online space, Amanda Frances, always says, "God is not mad at you for your desires[12]."

I'm not even religious, but I resonated with this deeply. I felt like I tiptoed around everyone in my life, hoping people wouldn't be mad at me or think that what I'm doing was "wrong". In psychology, we call this "moral perfectionism[13]", when a person is hyper fixated on being "good" and "right", therefore making them anxious and afraid of doing something wrong or being a bad person. When I was diagnosed with ADHD, I found out that morality was extremely important to neurodivergent folks, and I saw this trend of needing to be "good" in all areas of my life. This started off with my parents and other adults as a kid, and then in university with professors or older students. In jobs, it was my supervisors and superiors. With my business, it was coaches and mentors. And then finally, when I had worked through it all, I realized I was tiptoeing around the universe, too.

---

[12] *Rich as F*ck*, by Amanda Frances, 2021
[13] *Understanding Moral Perfectionism*, by Sophie Holoboff, 2020

I was afraid that my asking for more meant I was bad. That I was greedy or selfish, and I wouldn't be rewarded. I worked on a system of cause and effect - if I did this, then that would happen.

But deep down, my desires were linked to creating my own happiness and wellbeing. I wanted money so I could feel safe and live a freedom-filled life, and so I could give generously to those I love and those in need. But on the surface, my "wanting" of money felt bad because of what media and social programming had told me was bad, what religion had deemed evil or dishonourable, how patriarchy and misogyny skews society's view of women - and the wheels on the bus go round and round.

What is under the surface of *your* wants and needs? Do you desire a beautiful handbag because it makes you feel good? What happens when you feel good? What does the bag represent to you?

If we have a base belief of "I am bad", you don't question why you want what you want or why you do the things you do - you will just assume that the superficial reason is the only one there is. You assume that because you want the handbag, you want to look expensive and you want to appear rich, which makes you selfish and greedy and uncaring towards others. While this is a reality for some people, even though there are heaps of misogyny and negative views of money rolled into there - why does it have to be yours? Why can't you be a wonderful, caring human who likes designer shit?

A bad person who is scamming people and fraud-ing people does not worry about doing so. They are not consumed with thoughts about not being good enough, and they sure as hell aren't buying books to help better themselves.

When you neglect your own wants, needs, and desires because you believe they make you bad, you are unconsciously telling yourself that you shouldn't have them in the first place and therefore reinforcing that they are, in fact, bad.

You Are Just Enough, Even When You Are Too Much

We've already established that we are hypocritical and contradicting, and this is just another example of that - you are constantly vacillating between feeling not enough, and then worrying about being too much.

I would hit up against this with my online presence. I wanted to be good enough for my audience and for my clients. But when it began to happen, I would slink back into not enoughness - because the fear of being too much was extremely potent.

Too loud. Too big. Too opinionated. Too crass. Too smart. Too pretentious.

Historically, women have been regarded as sweet, caring, kind, and maternal when they are soft, quiet, and mysterious. They are secretly beautiful, whereas the girl that swears, has a loud voice, and talks too much is considered as deep as a puddle, and undesirable.

It is a running joke in my family. I'll sit next to my 88-year-old East Indian grandfather, and he'll tell me to get up and help in the kitchen, comment on how my swearing is unladylike, and say that my sister and I are being too loud (in everyone's defense, we are like, REALLY loud). My granddad is simultaneously proud of me for being an ambitious and successful businesswoman, while harping on the very characteristics that have made me that way.

Cultural and societal norms are beginning to change. **But the only way they change is when someone challenges them.**

What's behind the thought of being "too much" is the premise that you are the first (or the boldest) that this person has seen.

When I first started going to therapy, I'd try to talk to my parents about my mental health issues. While they are uberly supportive, they would also get very fucked up over Jilly, their smart, accomplished, and successful Jilly, potentially having some kind of internal struggles. They couldn't hold my emotions or my struggles - it was too much for them. I had to bravely talk about it more and more and more. Now, I am way more open with them and they receive it in such a better way.

But for a moment there, it was too much. And if I believed too much was bad, I'd never get to the place where everything I did and everything I am feels Enough.

You will only be too much when you are the first, or the boldest. You may also be worried about judgment, but only because *you* are judging someone who is seemingly "too much" in your eyes. This will be rectified by thinking back to those individuals, and wondering what you saw in them that you had never seen before.

Familiarity is safe to the brain. "I've seen this before" is safe to the brain. You might appear as "too much", but only because you are doing The Thing. You are taking up space. As you should. Life is too short to sit in the corner and wave away the compliments, the opportunities, and the times to shine. The more you do it, the more comfortable you become.

FACING FEEDBACK AND CRITICISM

A natural fear that will come from actively taking up space is the fear of being criticized. By keyboard warriors, trolls, your own flesh and blood, and well-meaning friends. Here's the thing - not everyone is qualified to give you feedback or criticize you.

Social media and the internet have allowed us to comment on basically anything and everything. This doesn't mean we *should,* it just means that we *can.*

You won't find me walking around a bank telling people how they should spend their money. I have no idea how they should spend their money. But if I'm in a room with my family, I *will* give my unsolicited opinion at all times. Because they're my family and we're all a little too honest with each other. If they choose to listen to me or not is completely up to them - I'm Gucci regardless.

Not everyone is qualified to give you their opinion, but some might give it to you anyway. And when you feel like a fraud and like you *don't* know best, you will internalize anything and everything. **This is a Choice.**

You are allowed to know what's best for you, and you are also allowed to hire out and seek advice from someone who you are trying to emulate or who you believe has what you want. Everyone else is just a spectator without full understanding and context.

Now, what if someone says something and it feels true? What if they criticize you and you think that they might be right?

It is still a decision *you* make to take inventory of what they said. You can do this without shame and with compassion - you are a work-in-progress, and it doesn't mean that you don't deserve success and love and all good things. It just means there's room for improvement in this particular area, and congratulations, that means you are a Human Doing Life. Nothing has gone wrong.

The truth is, you are going to disappoint people in your life. And that's because everyone has an expectation of how others should act. You have an expectation of how the Starbucks barista should act, and how your mother should act. Everything is seen through your lens of experience - and other people are no different. Meaning, you will absolutely disappoint others. You will think you're doing everything right and everything perfectly, and someone will still cast you as the villain in their tale.

They're going to be mad anyway. You cannot make a single decision that is going to appease everyone in your life at the same time. You can fly under the radar, making decisions and then cringing when you tell people, hoping their reaction won't send you spiraling into shame and self-loathing. Or, you could commit yourself to the very notion that they are just seeing your decision and your life through their own lens, and speaking from that experience.

The mistake you're making is inviting people to be conscious contributors instead of simple spectators. I used to do this by telling my family, friends, and partner anything and everything before I did it. I was unconsciously seeking approval and validation, but it only confused me more on what I really wanted. I remember telling my friends I wanted to call my coaching business "Roses are Red" because I wanted to be a Relationship Coach. They shot it down innocently, saying it was too specific. But with all the love in the world - what the fuck did they know? They were hearing me and being helpful. But where we ask for help *matters* when we're making decisions.

If they are not doing what you're doing, or if they do not have what you want - it is your choice to see them as a conscious contributor or as a simple spectator.

Okay wait, Jill - again, this is *my* responsibility to field everyone's opinions about my life?

Yes. It is always our responsibility to take what we hear and experience and make it mean something.

Make like the penguins in Madagascar - smile and wave boys, smile and wave. While others may give you their commentary, opinions, hot takes - it is within your rights to accept or reject it. You don't have to tell them you reject it. You can smile and nod while you think in your head "no fuckin way", like when a family member was trying to convince me to go into finance for university so I could get a secure job and I didn't have the heart to tell him I once was put in special education for math, because simple math is like reading hieroglyphics to me.

You get to be the chooser of your choices. This means taking responsibility for them as well - but you don't need to explain yourself to anybody who is committed to misunderstanding you. Let them have their lens of the world, and you will have yours.

But do you *really* know best? What if you don't know what's right for you and you're fucking it all up?

What if I told you that was just imposter syndrome, again, leading you to falsely believe that there is a right and a wrong, and you are doing it wrong - because that's all you've ever believed and been led to believe?

Don't Stay Small to Make Others Comfortable

There is a quiet knowing when someone is always there while you suffer, but never there when you celebrate.

And it has nothing to do with you.

Most people do not go after what they want. They stay stuck in fear of judgment, criticism, and ridicule. They balk at the people who are Doing the Thing, completely unaware that it's because their own insecurities are being uncovered.

These people may consciously or unconsciously try to keep you small. Be big anyways, and don't spend too much time on *why* they're doing so.

Because it has nothing to do with you.

When you shrink yourself, when you make yourself small - you are going against the natural state you're meant to be in. You go from listening to your intuition, to listening to your fear.

That temporary reprieve when you people-please by dimming your light, is not worth the disappointment and dissatisfaction of an unfulfilled purpose because of someone who doesn't see that they too can grab their worthiness with both hands and make something of themselves.

People are gonna talk shit, they're going to criticize everything you do, and they're going to give you their opinions - and a lot of the time it's not even strangers, it's people in your life that you often see.

You don't need to cut them out and tell everyone on TikTok that your grandma's toxic. You can stand true in your purpose, follow your heart, and only share your biggest aspirations and dreams with people who will cheer you on.

Here I am again, making a reference Brené Brown[14] - but if they're not in the arena putting up the good fight for themselves, they don't get to cast a shadow on the light bursting out of you.

And even if they try - for the last time, it truly has *nothing* to do with you.

---

[14] *Daring Greatly, by Brené Brown, 2012*

This, or Something Better

I have a confession to make.

While I used to be supremely negative and sarcastic, something I have always believed is that everything was working out for me.

In high school, I believed I'd be accepted to the schools I wanted, and that I would make the right decision.

In university, I believed that I'd pass a class, even if I was having a rough go. I even wrote "Please help me pass this course and I'll never take another one ever again" on my final philosophy exam in my first year of university, and the professor passed me with a 50. Which is ironic, because what I do now is basically modern-day philosophy. I hope wherever that professor is, she got her good karma for passing me.

Throughout my government career, I believed that timing was everything and that an opportunity wouldn't pass me by that wasn't meant for me. I did well in interviews, got the jobs I wanted, and it seemed as though everything always worked out for me.

It's kind of like when I was a kid and I'd talk to God in our front yard. We weren't religious, and I had no understanding of religion or spirituality. But I stated what I wanted and what I needed.

I've always believed that if something didn't work out, it was for the best - no matter how much it hurt or what the circumstances were.

This, or something better.

Believing this is merely *accepting* what is instead of *resisting* what is. If you've felt like everything is a push and pull between what's happening for you internally and externally - may I introduce to you, the very thought of "What if this was okay?"

Earlier, we talked about the acceptance of self. In a world where we are taught to either love or hate our bodies, stand up for one thing unabashedly or stay in the shadows, I have spent most of my time here helping you feel okay with being on middle, neutral ground...right?

So if you can accept yourself and that can spiral a whole journey back home to your worthiness...you can accept the circumstances of life, as well - and you may find yourself happier than ever.

They are one in the same. Acceptance of yourself means you are not fighting against what is, and that will eventually bleed into your life. You are not thinking you're too old, or that you missed an opportunity, or that you can't be happy unless you get that next thing.

Because the thing you're actually chasing is contentment. You want the house so you can sit on your couch and watch Gilmore Girls, marveling at how you made a home for yourself. You want a job so you can get that steady paycheck and feel proud of yourself and buy Starbucks every Friday morning.

Contentment feels safe. Stable. A sure thing. Certain.

And there's also room for more. If you so choose.

This scarce feeling of "I'm not where I need to be, I don't have what I want, this isn't it" means that there is never enough. Another version of imposter syndrome, thinking that enough is a metric by which we can measure ourselves and our lives. But as I've said in previous chapters - enough doesn't actually exist. It is always what we're making it mean.

When we seek out contentment and then accept life (and ourselves) for what it is, there is a tiny whisper that goes, "Now what?"

Not in a boring way. In a way that you have it all - and now, you have room for more.

Not only can you recognize contentment with your thoughts, but your nervous system craves it. When your nervous system is activated by way of stress responses, you are like a glass of water that is always spilling over the edge. Any little shake to the glass causes you to spill over - the sensitivity and rawness is REAL. Everything feels like it's going to push you over the edge.

Another thing that happens when you're in a stress response is that you can only ever focus on what you can experience with your senses (AKA what's tangible and on the physical plane of this Earth). So when we're talking about manifesting our desires and creating amazing lives, it can be a little hard to do that when we're always stressed and therefore always focused on the only things we can see, touch, and hear in our current reality. As Dr. Joe Dispenza talks about in his research of the brain and the subconscious mind, the way we create better, new things in our future, is to stop reliving and recreating our past[15].

When you slow down enough to be in the present moment, to notice how you *actually* feel, experience sensation, attune your body to the now... the nervous system regulates and absorbs what's being poured into it. You create new neural pathways from this place. You can actually take in what is being offered to you in a whole, healthy way. You leave so much more room for abundance and joy - because your emotional resilience is strong.

So what does this look like in the everyday?

How is right now good enough?

How are you, right now, good enough?

What can you accept today?

I want to also mention that acceptance of the present is not giving up on the future. Rather, it is just another way you are certain.

When you are accepting of where you're at, it's because you are sure that things are going to work out. You are certain that what you want, wants you. It becomes less about forcing.

This doesn't negate hard work and effort. Of course, you have to work towards your dreams. But the energy of "I know this is going to work out for me. This, or something better" is a lot different than "I have to put all of effort and time and work into this to make it happen. I *need* this to happen exactly how I envision it".

Acceptance of where you are and what is, is so much harder when you don't accept and love yourself. That's why it's the

---

[15] *Becoming Supernatural*, by Dr. Joe Dispenza, 2019

first step. Because acceptance of your life and where it is now, is only made possible through acceptance of who you are.

FEELING WORTHY IS AN ONGOING IDENTITY CRISIS

Belief in yourself and self-acceptance = worthiness. But it also means you are more apt to go after the things you want, take more risks, and put yourself out there.

This is scary. This is uncomfortable.

It is *uncomfortable* to declare what you want, especially to yourself. Because then, you have the troubling experience of either making it happen, or being disappointed.

Near the beginning of this book, we discussed the Conscious Critical Faculty; a filter in your brain that negates information based on if you've seen or experienced something before.

When we are uplevelling our worthiness game, there is a process that happens:

We are unaware and unconscious of what's possible → we become aware of what other people have achieved → we believe it's possible for them but not for us.

This is where a lot of people stop. They decide, "That can happen for them, but not for me". They believe their perceived limitations, they believe their own thoughts *alone* would never be able to achieve the goal they want, and then they carry on with their lives.

In actuality, there is *always* a next step to whatever path you're on. You might start off believing that it's not possible for you - and remember, unworthiness is a rite of passage. It's totally normal and okay.

But then, you can begin opening yourself up to the possibility of achieving that thing, too.

Years ago, when I was working in HR at a production plant that my Dad worked at for a summer job between university years, I stumbled upon a YouTube video where the couple was in the Maldives. It looked *so* fancy - villas over the water, breakfast in the infinity pool, snorkeling in the Indian ocean. I had never heard of this place before, and my brain did its thing - became aware of it, and told myself I'd never be able to afford a trip like that - at least, not on my own.

It wasn't until years later, with my own business, that I entertained that next step. What if I *could* go to the Maldives? I wonder how much it is? What if it was a honeymoon spot for my fiancé and I?

What if, what if, what if.

Identifying as someone who is worthy to have the thing you want always starts with *curiosity*.

Your brain is a sensitive little peach because of your conscious critical faculty. You can't run at it with brand new information it's never seen before and demand that it become accustomed to that thing immediately. You'll introduce the concept to yourself and see how it fits into your life and what you want for yourself. You'll open your mind up to receiving that thing and what that would mean for you and your life.

If I wanted to believe we could go to the Maldives, I had to get curious - how much should we save for it, when would we go, what extras would we get, what would it mean for us to spend X amount of money on a vacation...

It might just sound like a vacation to you. But to me, going on a luxurious trip across the world IS a lesson in worthiness. We could just go to Mexico for $1000 each and call it a day. But a trip like this means something - about what I think I deserve and what I decide I can have.

Step 1: Work on your worthiness and your ability to feel deserving.

Step 2: Introduce everything you want to achieve/receive with curiosity.

Step 3: Actively play in the energy of what it would be like for that to be a reality for you.

Becoming The Worthy Woman

Becoming the Worthy Woman is really just becoming the best/highest version of yourself.

It is not just the version of you that has what they want - but they are the **person** who has those things.

The problem with most goal-setting practices is that it's mainly focused on everything that is external to us. We think about the house we would have, the job we would have, and all the cool things that we can touch with our hands and see with our eyes.

But what actually *creates* those things are your thoughts and your feelings. A friend once shared a quote with me that goal-setting is never about actually achieving the goal, it's about who you're becoming in the process of achieving that goal. Because once the goal is achieved - it's time for another one. What you are really seeking is the fulfillment, the empowering thoughts, and the safe feelings of achieving the goal. You want to reap the rewards of the goal, yes, like buying a house and enjoying that house. But you're not just going to stop achieving and doing things once you buy a home.

Your drive for fulfillment, success, and achievement is not a problem - but how you see yourself and how you feel as you do it are more important than you even realize. When you're achieving for worth, you are in pain because you believe that your worth comes AFTER the achievement - but you were *always* worthy. You were *always* good enough. Goals, achievements, projects, jobs - these are all things that we *do* so we feel purposeful. But it is no fun to achieve and do and accomplish when we hate ourselves. It makes the job 10x harder and zaps the energy and joy out of everything we do.

And think about it this way - when you think about achieving something, you have a happy version of yourself in your mind. If you were to visualize yourself achieving this goal, you'd probably see yourself smiling and feeling good and feeling *proud* of yourself. So of course, when you do achieve the things, it makes sense why you've been feeling unsatisfied and unworthy - because you focused too much on the *doing*, and not enough on the *being*.

So how do you become **The Worthy Woman**?

Complete the following exercise:

Pick a goal you're working towards. Write it down.

Imagine you've achieved it as the highest version of yourself:

What does the highest version of yourself *think* about herself?

How does the highest version of yourself *feel* everyday? What does she do so she feels that way?

What habits/routines does she participate in?

What does she think about her past mistakes/failures?

How does she speak to herself?

Now, on a separate piece of paper, answer those same questions, but instead of imagining your highest self, write down what you *currently* think about yourself, how you *currently* feel everyday, what you *currently* do, your *current* habits/routines, what you *currently* think about your past mistakes/failures, and how you *currently* speak to yourself.

And put those two pieces of paper together. See the differences.

And start becoming her, now.

*You can find this exercise at www.jillianparekh.com/yns-book - it is called Your Worthy Woman Identity.

Beliefs You Can Borrow to Lily Pad Your Way to Worthiness

1. What's for me won't miss me.
2. I believe in my capacity to handle whatever is thrown my way.
3. Wanting it means it's meant for me.
4. I am worthy of every opportunity presented to me.
5. The universe is always looking out for me.
6. I have a message worth shouting from the rooftops.

How to Be A Sensitive Bad Bitch

1. Don't be afraid of your feelings. If you can feel it all, you can have it all.

2. Know the difference between something you need to stand up to, and something that triggers your healing. Be responsive, not reactive.

3. Remember that everyone is looking at you and your life from their own lens of experience. No offence, but they don't know shit about fuck when it comes to you and your life. You are the captain of your ship. Trust yourself.

4. You've made it through all of your hard days.

5. Every emotion is temporary; good and bad.

6. You are never too much of anything. You are the perfect amount.

7. Everything is either a blessing or lesson.

8. It's all happening *for* you, not *to* you.
9. Throw yourself a pity party and then get back to work.
10. Forgiveness is for you.

Your Journey to Worthiness Begins Today

Your journey to worthiness begins today, right now, as you are.

And when you fall short, forget who you are, fuck up, fail, stumble, make a mistake - the journey continues.

Overcoming imposter syndrome and stepping into your worthiness means that at every new level, new experience, new skill, new *whatever* - you will be faced with the same questions:

Can I do this?

Will it work for me?

Am I capable?

My grandma and granddad live in the country near an abandoned train track. The weeds have overgrown amongst the tracks, and people barely yield at the stop sign anymore because it's assumed that the train tracks are no longer in use. But they're still there.

Your old stories and old beliefs are the same way. They may be overgrown with weeds in your subconscious mind, but the option is always there to choose them again. The option is always there to allow them to light up and be in use - the tracks of the mind are familiar. They are comfortable. They are what you used to believe yourself to be.

When you see your worthiness, you begin to see that there are other routes to take. Other paths to walk. Other adventures that you never saw coming.

But the *option* to revert is always there, especially when we feel negative emotions. Remember, emotions can't hurt you even though we avoid them like they can. They might physically hurt, but they are not as dangerous as our brain makes them out to be. If you can hold discomfort, process your emotions without making them mean anything, and continue believing in your value, your worth, and what you can accomplish - you have won the lottery of life.

Predictive Avoidance is a term I made up for my coaching clients, for what I describe as thinking you can see into your future and you know what feeling is coming, so you avoid the behaviors or actions that would bring on that feeling.

How often do you do this? How often do you automatically think "I'm not doing that" because your brain has already jumped ahead to your inevitable fate of feeling shitty?

I used to do this with social events *(and still catch myself doing it sometimes because I'm a human)*. Thinking about going to events where I don't know everyone and would potentially have to introduce myself gives me SO much anxiety, because I stutter and I have a lifetimes' worth of embarrassment and shame from getting stuck on my name and people laughing at me, giving me weird looks, and etc.

Embarrassment and shame are heavy emotions, yes. Emotions that can kill me? No. When I avoid the social event that I would absolutely go to if I didn't have this fear, I'm not truly living out my purpose or living in alignment with what I want. I tell myself I have to sacrifice and suffer. When I go anyways and risk the embarrassment and shame, knowing that I can process it and move on from it without dying, I am living in alignment and with my highest good in mind.

It doesn't always feel good. Truthfully, being my highest self feels uncomfortable a lot of the time. But if I don't learn how to experience and process negative emotions, I don't allow myself to hold the discomfort of joy, purpose, play, elation, and fun, either.

Yes, holding discomfort does not always mean negative discomfort. Have you let yourself sit with being successful? With having a lot of money in your bank account? When good things happen, do you shy away? Does your brain automatically self-sabotage when you start to feel good and safe and okay?

You get to have good things.

You get to be happy.

You get to feel elated.

You get to dream.

It is uncomfortable for us to get what we want. We are in a society of hustle and grind and a culture of learning *how* to reach our goals - but what happens when we have them? We're onto the next one. The next thing that we are sure will make us feel the way we want to feel.

You get to feel whatever you want to feel, right now. You don't have to wait.

Earlier this year, I experimented with feeling proud of myself. We are all told to be humble, not to brag or boast. I have clear memories of my best friend in 10th grade making me feel stupid for celebrating a good play in flag football. I was conditioned, in a million other ways, to downplay and minimize the light inside of me, instead of letting it light me up and light the way for others, too.

So whenever I would visualize, I would try to tap into the feelings and would always feel pride. I would be so proud of myself when I left my stable government job to take my business full-time. I'd feel so proud of myself when I hit my first $100K. I'd feel so proud of myself when I made multiple 6-figures. I'd feel so proud of myself when I got engaged to my fiancé.

But in my day-to-day life, I wasn't cultivating the feeling of pride. I was waiting for the experience to allow myself to feel it.

You only ever work towards something for the feeling it gives you. Because when you die, there is nothing you take with you but how you felt and the experiences you had.

If I wanted to feel proud of myself when I achieved something, I had to learn what pride felt like in my body and I had to learn how to *hold* pride, even if it felt uncomfortable. I had to learn how to dispel the stories and the beliefs that told me I shouldn't feel proud of myself.

Because then, when the tangible goal manifests in my reality, I recognize the feeling. I *know* how I'm supposed to feel, and I allow myself to feel it.

Do you allow things to be good? Do you allow yourself to relax, to rest, to feel worthy?

Do this exercise: Sit back and close your eyes. Breathe in a big breath into the belly, and then exhale out of your nose. What does it feel like to feel worthy? To have all the things you want? How will you feel when that happens? Does your mind jump to all the things you have to organize, do, buy, etcetera?

What if you quieted the mind and just allowed yourself to *hold* what you have. Hold your worthiness with both hands. Maybe even imagine you're in bed at the end of the day, not thinking about what you have to do tomorrow, but just holding your worthiness and holding everything you've achieved.

Do you allow yourself to hold things with both hands? To experience things in the present moment? To just be here now?

Your journey to worthiness never ends, my friend. It is a moment-to-moment experience of choosing and deciding and being with yourself.

The Good Avocados

My Omi is my maternal grandmother. She was just a toddler when World War II began, and her family was a part of the Exodus of Germans to Poland. She lived a very scarce, impoverished, and brutal beginning of her life, and I am so grateful to be a part of her lineage.

My Omi and my maternal step-grandfather, Johnny, now live in a beautiful home and did extremely well for themselves; however, Omi always talks about how because she grew up so poor, when she came to Canada in the 60s, she promised herself she'd never be poor again. But that didn't look like relishing in the abundance she has - instead, she still *feels* as if everything could go away at any moment.

How often do we promise ourselves that nothing bad will ever happen again by reliving how it used to feel, as a means to protect ourselves from feeling too good and letting it slip through our fingers?

Omi once said to me that she doesn't even buy the good avocados at the store. And it had me thinking - how often do we deny ourselves the joy of the present moment because of a past feeling?

Because I felt unworthy of the present moment, I was always wishing for the future and living in the past. I would save outfits, bottles of nice champagne, make-up, jewellry, and other things that were celebrations of joy and my higher self - all for another day, a future day. Because of my anxiety and feelings of unworthiness, I never felt good enough here, so I wanted to be there.

But as we've learned throughout this book, There is only created from Here. All we have is now, and a surefire way to recreate the past is by thinking the past being repeated is inevitable. What if we gave that same energy to creating something new?

Our past and who we've been stops us from believing that we are worthy of receiving right now, as we are.

If you don't allow yourself to dream, it's probably because you just believe what you want won't happen for you, and you're participating in that predictive avoidance we talked about earlier so you don't feel disappointed.

If you *do* allow yourself to dream but nothing in your current reality is changing, it's probably because you're disconnected from your highest self - you see her, you see the life you want, but there's a safe distance between the two of you because you're so caught up in who you've been that there's no room for the creation of who you can become.

So firstly, identifying what thoughts and beliefs are holding you back from stepping into your highest self is a good place to start. And then, you can work on actually *receiving* what you were always worthy of having.

Receiving is a big part of worthiness. Being receptive to the abundance you seek is just as important as being in the process of creating it. This means noticing when things are beginning to happen instead of discounting it. Being grateful for what's manifesting and holding the vibration of it, knowing more is on the way. "Thank you, more please" is one of my favourite affirmations whenever I receive *anything* that I want more of.

And this also means you need to get comfortable with being receptive to your own sense of worthiness. Receiving a compliment. Feeling proud of yourself. Taking the credit. Taking up space. Being seen. Not shutting someone down when they want to help you or give you something. When good things happen to you, not letting your mind reject them or talk you out of not receiving it.

The thing about the good avocados is that you have to decide to buy them. You have to allow yourself to have them. You can ask the universe for what you want, and they can show up in your reality - but you are in control of having them and holding them, which is directly associated to how worthy you feel.

You're worthy of the good avocados *right now*.

It's All Happening

It's all happening, even when it feels like it's not.

There is a difference between action taken from hope and action taken from belief.

When actions are taken from hope, they feel like tiptoes. They are too quiet, they are under the radar, they are unconfident. They are plan B and C and D and E.

When actions are taken from belief, they feel like leaps. They are bold, assertive, confident. They are certain. They may not always feel *good,* but they always feel *right.*

Hope *wavers.*

Belief **sticks.**

Question #1: What do you currently believe about yourself?

Question #2: What do you *want* to believe about yourself?

Work on unlearning and releasing Question #1, and tapping into and embodying Question #2.

And the entire time, believe that it's all happening for you. Because it is, if that's what you believe.

You Are Good Enough

When your inner imposter tries to say that you're not good enough, this is what you need to remember:

Your brain is just running a program, a pattern you've always been used to repeating. It's not an actual indication of what you're capable of.

The voice inside your head that automatically goes "NOPE" whenever there's an opportunity for your worthiness to be tested?

You get to decide whether or not you give it to the microphone.

Remember that you can't always choose your first thought, but you can choose your second.

I'm not good enough is just a program your brain is used to running.

Will you decide to break the cycle?

Will you choose differently?

All you have to be is open - open to the possibility of being good enough. Of having more to say. Of being worthy of what you want.

You are good enough.

And...

You Get to Decide That You're Good Enough

It won't matter what you accomplish or what you do - you cannot be perfect enough to fit everyone else's idea of worthy.

But you can be the perfect fit for what *you* believe is worthy.

Meaning - you get to decide that you're good enough, right now, as you are. I've taught you how to start thinking different thoughts, how to forgive yourself for your past and stop shaming yourself, how to feel your feelings without making them mean anything, and how to believe that you're worthy of good things.

None of it will matter if you don't decide, right now, that you're enough.

Whatever you decide you are, that is what you are. And that is why you've read this book, despite any external success you have - because you don't *think* or *feel* it.

But you get to decide. And it is a choice, to wake up and

choose worthiness. Like Britney Spears in her Lucky music video - you can have everything in the world, and *still* feel like you're not enough.

You are worthy of deciding you're worthy. You don't need to wait for anyone to validate you, or to achieve the goal you're certain will make you good enough.

You can decide, right now, that you're good enough.

Now What?

Now, it's time for you to decide on what you want, and go get it.

Sit down and make a list, titling it "Dreams and Desires". If you knew you couldn't fail, and if you were the most Worthy version of yourself (think back to the Worthy Woman exercise), what would you want to do with your life? What would you be calling in from the universe, like an Amazon order?

Remember - when those inevitable thoughts of "I can't have that, that won't happen for me" come up, accompanied by the feeling of not enoughness - remember that this is normal, you are safe, it is just a program, and it is your job to introduce this dream/desire into your realm of possibility, taking action on it bit-by-bit, until it becomes a full blown reality.

Your dreams and desires are there because you're supposed to have them. Your work is to do what you need to do to achieve and receive them, and that work includes how you think and feel about yourself.

Everything you want is meant for you. So pick a goal, match

your identity to the person who has that goal, and go the fuck after it.

Welcome Home

You're not special.

The universe isn't leaving you out.

There is more than enough abundance available for you.

And you get to have it.

You get to have all of it, simply because you exist.

You're enough.

You have always been enough.

You just needed to remember.

Welcome home.

Acknowledgements

Thank you for reading my very first book, like ever. Holy shit, I wrote a book! I self-published it, too. Go, me.

Make sure to download all the resources and exercises from this book at www.jillianparekh.com/yns-book

If you want to take this work with me deeper, follow me on Instagram or TikTok, and visit my website www.jillianparekh.com for my coaching offers.

You can find me on YouTube at Jillian Parekh Coaching where I upload videos and meditations.

You can listen to my podcast, The From Imposter to Empowered Podcast.

Thank you to my family and best friends for always believing in me and encouraging my work. Being an entrepreneur doesn't always make sense to those outside of it - but I am grateful that the ones that matter cheer me on regardless.

Thank you to my fiancé, Dustin, for saying, "Wow, that's cool" every time I hit a new page limit, and for agreeing to read it even if it takes him a hundred years. I love you soooo much and couldn't do any of this without you.

Thank you to my business community, my audience, my coaching clients, and my mentors for inspiring me and leading me towards a path I never could have even dreamt for myself.

And lastly, as the great Snoop Dogg[16] once said - "I want to thank me. I want to thank me for believing in me. I want to thank me for doing all this hard work. I want to thank me for never quitting."

It is so easy to reject yourself and give up on yourself so the world can't do it first. And I struggle with imposter syndrome HARD - but when I practiced the philosophies, concepts, and exercises that are in this book, it helped me come home to the fact that I am good enough, have always been good enough, and am just as capable as the next bitch of having the life and business that I want.

So, I want to acknowledge myself, and you should acknowledge yourself, too. Because people can rally around and support you, but no one else is going to believe in you *for* you, and they can't take the action for you, either. Actions come from our thoughts, mostly about ourselves - so take care of them, take care of you, and come home to your innate and inherent worthiness. It has always been there, you just needed to remember.

I love you.

Your Coach, Jill

---

[16] *Hollywood Walk of Fame Acceptance Speech by Snoop Dogg, 2018*

Sources

1. Feel like a fraud? *American Psychological Association, 2013*
2. Cognitive Dissonance Theory by *Saul McLeod*, 2018
3. The SharpBrains Guide to Brain Fitness by *Fernandez, Michelon, and Chapman*, 2013
4. The Conscious Critical Faculty, *Terence Watts*
5. How Confirmation Bias Works, by *Iqra Noor*, 2020
6. Thought Field Therapy and its derivatives: Rapid relief of mental health problems through tapping on the body, by *Phil Mollon*, 2007
7. 90 Seconds to Emotional Resilience by *Alyson M. Stone*, 2019
8. Breaking the Habit of Being Yourself by *Dr. Joe Dispenza*, 2013
9. The Imposter Phenomenon, *International Journal of Behavioral Science*, 2011
10. The Secret Thoughts of Successful Women, *Dr. Valerie Young*, 2011
11. What is an Example of the Dunning-Kruger Effect? By

Divya Jacob, 2021

12. Oprah Reflects by *Daily Post Staff*, 2011
13. Rich as F*ck, by *Amanda Frances*, 2021
14. Understanding Moral Perfectionism, by *Sophie Holoboff*, 2020
15. Daring Greatly, by *Brené Brown*, 2012
16. Becoming Supernatural, by *Dr. Joe Dispenza*, 2019
17. Hollywood Walk of Fame Acceptance Speech by *Snoop Dogg*, 2018

www.ingramcontent.com/pod-product-compliance
Lightning Source LLC
Chambersburg PA
CBHW050233120526
44590CB00016B/2072